The Origins of Freemasonry

The ORIGINS of FREEMASONRY

Facts & Fictions

MARGARET C. JACOB

UNIVERSITY OF PENNSYLVANIA PRESS

Philadelphia

10 9 8 7 6 5 4 3 2 1

Published by
University of Pennsylvania Press
Philadelphia, Pennsylvania 19104-4112

Library of Congress Cataloging-in-Publication Data

Jacob, Margaret C., 1943–
    The origins of freemasonry : facts & fictions / Margaret C. Jacob.
        p.   cm.
    ISBN-13: 978-0-8122-3901-0
    ISBN-10: 0-8122-3901-6 (cloth : alk. paper)
    Includes bibliographical references and index.
    1. Freemasonry—History.   I. Title.
HS403 .J28   2005
366'.1—dc22   2005042440

To the memory of the late Beitj Croiset van Uchelen (d. 1996),
librarian of the archives and library of the Grand East of The Netherlands,
and to its superb collection, located at the Cultural Masonic Center
"Prins Frederik," 9, Jan Evertstraat, The Hague, one
of the finest collections in masonic history; open to all scholars.

CONTENTS

Introduction

In 2004 a best-selling novel, *The Da Vinci Code*, by Dan Brown told readers that the freemasons were descended from the Knights Templar. It is a great story, and as the author makes clear, part of a work of fiction. Somehow these fictions pass into fact. In November of the same year, Disney Productions released a feature film, *National Treasure*, about how the founding fathers left behind secret buried treasure. They were prone to secrecy because they were freemasons. Another great story, this one partly true. Some of the founding fathers, like George Washington and Benjamin Franklin, were freemasons. Before 2004 was out, people would be asking why the freemasons liked to bury treasure. In the late 1990s a furor erupted in Britain with enemies of the freemasons claiming that masonic policemen released criminals if they belonged to the order. To counter this bad press, a devotee wrote a history of freemasonry in which he claimed that they were descended from a group of reformers in the seventeenth century who called themselves Rosicrucians.[1] No evidence was offered for that fictive story, but the author did at least cast a cold eye on the story about the freemasons and the Knights Templar. Separating masonic facts from masonic fictions can be difficult.

As a historian who has written about eighteenth-century freemasonry, I get asked all the time—even by the company doing the film for Disney Productions—if the freemasons descended from the medieval Knights Templar, if the eye and triangle on the back of the American dollar bill was meant to be masonic, and not least, what are the secrets so guarded by the freemasons? This book attempts to answer some of those questions by looking at the first century of freemasonry, at its

FIGURE 1. Let us join him. This angel is knocking on the temple door for the secrets found in the anonymous "exposure," the frontispiece to *De Metselaar ontmomd* [sic], *of het rechte geheim der vryemetselaaren ontdekt . . . 1753* (Arnhem: Jacob Nyhoff). With permission from the masonic library, Prins Frederik Cultural Masonic Center, The Hague; copyright Grand East of the Netherlands.

FIGURE 2. George Washington's masonic apron. With permission of the Masonic Library and Museum of Pennsylvania, Philadelphia.

founding decades in eighteenth-century Europe. Reading about that history should dispel the notion about the Knights Templar as the origin of the masonic movement. But it should do more. Historical understanding asks readers to try to imagine what men like George Washington, Benjamin Franklin, Paul Revere, General Lafayette, and

Voltaire (admitted late in life), Mozart, and the German poet Goethe might have found appealing in their masonic lodges.

I want to remove the veil from a secret society that turns out not to be very secret at all. I want to read the original European books and archives from the eighteenth century and see what thousands of men—among them, in the colonies, our founding fathers—and a few thousand women saw, what ideals the lodges sought to impart, what activities they promoted. I want to get closer to actual lives, but also to larger questions about the political implications of masonic membership. How did a private society dedicated to equality and fraternity cope with the pressures coming from a deeply hierarchical society, that was also increasingly dominated by market transactions, by wealth as distinct from birth. Those pressures mirror the tensions inherent in modern democracies, between the ideals of equality and the messy reality of status, wealth, privilege, and day-to-day inequality.

Much of what this book reveals depends upon European sources. American freemasonry derived directly from its British counterpart (as imported by Benjamin Franklin), and going back to the source of it all makes the most sense. I am also trained as a European and not an American historian, and I have not walked the archival terrain in the American libraries of the East Coast, the way I have in Europe. For the American side of the story, a fuller account can be found in the superb book by Steven Bullock, *Revolutionary Brotherhood*.[2]

Perhaps American readers of this book will also be drawn to it because civic life at present seems so relatively impoverished. We join fewer groups; the average rate of membership in civic organizations is about one-tenth as large today as it was thirty years ago.[3] Voluntary associations that radically crossed class lines have largely disappeared, replaced by advocacy groups or professional associations.[4] We may rightly marvel at a time when joining something like a lodge meant a commitment that could be life-long and that challenged assumptions about who could call himself a "brother," someone who met with others, "upon the level," to use the masonic phrase. The need for entertainment, stimulation, possibly an escape from rigidity in clan and chapel, led some eighteenth century men—and women—to seek the fellowship of freemasonry. This was true for American whites and blacks. For the latter, black lodges offered the possibility of self-governance. Documenting the history of masonic lodges in the old and new worlds of the eighteenth century can, however, be difficult. In some cases old world lodges felt that what they were doing was so important that historical records needed to be carefully preserved. But other lodges, especially those for—and then by—women left only traces.

Over the years I have visited just about every masonic library in western Europe. In the 1970s I started this search for the historical reality of freemasonry by asking for permission to begin where the original lodges began, in London in the 1690s. I wrote to the Library of the Grand Lodge of Great Britain, in Freemasons' Hall on Great Queen Street, right in the heart of Soho, and requested permission to visit and read in its manuscript archives. The answer was a flat "no." Why? Because at that time the records were closed to all nonmasons. In response I pointed out that, unlike many European Grand Lodges, the British one would not admit women as freemasons. Hence, with impeccable logic, I pleaded that the rule should not apply to me. They never answered that letter.

Times have changed, especially for British freemasons. Now all scholars have access to their library, everything is open. The early history of how English and Scottish guilds of stonemasons evolved into the freemasons of the eighteenth century is still incomplete, but in broad outline the story is now basically understood. The Scottish records as early as the 1650s show local guilds in need of cash admitting relatives, or prominent figures with philosophical interests who were non-masons. This process began as early as the sixteenth century, and one aspect of it must have been the intellectual interests of Scottish masons. The masters among them, like master masons elsewhere, knew geometry and acted in effect like architects. They were also steeped in the mysticism commonplace to the Renaissance, a tradition that imag-

FIGURE 3. Engraving from *De Almanack der Vrye Metzelaaren . . . 1780* (Amsterdam: Willem Coertze, Jr.), showing a young man who seeks admission to the lodge, brought blindfolded before those who will soon be his brothers. His chest is bare to prove he is a man and he is about to initiated into the "secrets" of the order. The master of the lodge sits waiting to receive him. The habit of revealing in print what was supposedly secret appears early in the history of freemasonry. With permission of the masonic library, Prins Frederik Cultural Masonic Center, The Hague; copyright Grand East of the Netherlands.

ined arts like architecture and alchemy provided clues to the underlying principles of nature. Among the earliest Scottish records—so brilliantly illuminated by David Stevenson—we see all of these traditions attracting learned gentlemen, some also drawn to the new science.[5]

The most interesting question raised by the process of converting lodges of stonemasons into enclaves of literate gentlemen, educated professionals, and a few tradesmen concerns not the breakdown of the exclusivity of the guilds under the pressure of market forces, but rather why so many men who had never lifted a brick wanted to join. Why did freemasonry become so respectable, or controversial, and spread to every country where Westerners had colonies? What was it that made freemasonry so appealing that we reckon its membership in the tens of thousands by 1750—and that included perhaps a thousand women. By 1780 there was barely a French town that did not have a lodge, and prominent and well-educated men and some women flocked to them. The growth of the lodges happened even in Catholic countries like France, despite the 1738 decree from Rome that prohibited Catholics from being freemasons. Taking Europe and America as a whole by 1789—the year of the French Revolution—well over a hundred thousand men had taken the masonic oath to the Grand Architect of the universe. There were more than four hundred lodges in Britain alone. A set of values and practices must have appealed across geographic, religious, and class barriers.

Getting answers to the questions about the appeal of daily life as a freemason, as well as about their political and economic attitudes and values, meant visiting even more masonic libraries. In Europe I quickly discovered that other, far more sinister visitors, had preceded me. In 1940, when the Nazis invaded the Low Countries and France, within twenty four hours they burst into the libraries and archives of the freemasons and confiscated all their records. They believed in the existence of a Jewish-Masonic conspiracy that sought to rule in every country through secrecy and corruption. The confiscated records were sent back to Berlin, where Hitler had set up an entire institute to research the contours of the conspiracy and reveal it to the world.[6] In the occupied countries elaborate exhibitions were opened in the confiscated masonic buildings. They were meant to show the nature of the enemy faced by the Germans, who put up pictures of Churchill, the king of England, and Roosevelt in masonic garb. Many now-aged Dutch and French freemasons whom I have met in these libraries joined the Resistance and the lodges so that they could be just like Churchill and Roosevelt (who were indeed freemasons). Getting at the eighteenth-century history of the lodges and their appeal meant cutting through a century or more of fictions about the freemasons as conspiratorial, or anti-Christian, or just corrupt and degenerate.

The story of Nazi confiscation and antimasonic propaganda has a bizarre ending. In 1945 the Russian army seized the contents of the Berlin institute and shipped it back to Moscow. There the records stayed hidden, until finally in the late 1990s the Putin government, burdened by debt to the European countries, agreed to return them.

Beginning in 2000, with more still to come, huge trucks journeyed from Moscow to Paris, Brussels, and The Hague, returning the lost masonic treasures. By far the largest shipment went to the French free-masons, and it is now possible to see new records about Franklin's masonic activities in Paris during the 1780s, or to trace the history of freemasonry in entire cities, like Bordeaux, long thought lost forever in 1940. Yet, make no mistake about it, the Jewish-masonic conspiracy theory lurks in far-right, often fascist ideologies still extant, although largely purged from European and American hate-mongering. *The Protocols of the Elders of Zion* (1897), the ground-zero text of twentieth-century anti-Semitism, devoted a chapter to the Jewish-masonic con-spiracy and thousands of copies continue to circulate, largely in the Middle East.[7]

In America, freemasonry has on the whole been far less controversial than in Europe. In Boston in the 1920s freemasons openly paraded, and many a small town's July 4 parade would be disappointing without the local lodge proudly atop their float. But in Europe during the eigh-teenth century powerful forces found freemasonry threatening. The lodges were a British import and often seen as instruments of British foreign policy. The Catholic Church spied in the lodges an alternative religion, and it disapproved of the lodge practice of holding frequent elections. That smacked of republicanism, not the absolute monarchies so beloved by the Church.

Making matters even more complicated, the freemasons themselves took in myths and fables and proclaimed them as true history. Freemasonry, they claimed, began at the building of Solomon's Temple. Late in the eighteenth century, freemasons looked back to the medieval Knights Templar and the shadowy Rosicrucians of the seventeenth century, assuming that if they had been secret then modern freemasons must be descended from them. The illogic persists among freemasons and their few remaining enemies—as well as untutored devotees—in the West. My task in the pages that follow is to separate out the myths and fictions, however charming, from what the historical records can tell us.

In chapter 1 I will take a general approach to the phenomenon of eighteenth-century freemasonry, to get its chronology straight and clear away some of the debris left from stories about the Knights Templar, the Rosicrucians, and other shadowy groups. Chapter 2 will try to get closer to what living as a freemason may have meant. Masonic almanacs and pocket diaries will be examined for what they can tell us about their users, or at the very least what the publishers of such items thought would please masonic brothers and sisters as consumers. In chapter 3 the extraordinary tendency of the lodges to become interested in how to govern will take center stage. All lodges claimed to admit according to merit, not birth or wealth. They focused on secret passwords, rituals, and a great deal of merrymaking. But willy-nilly, and oftentimes unselfconsciously, they proceeded to set up governments in microcosm, complete with elections, officers, and taxes.

However interested in new forms of governance, freemasons nonetheless had to live in the real world. Chapter 4 will explore how the masonic claim of being a fraternity that was a meritocracy worked in a market—and money-drive—society that was also deeply hierarchical. At the core of that chapter are plaintive letters of the 1780s from French brothers and sisters sent into the Grand Lodge of France, asking—sometimes demanding, other times begging—for charitable assistance. Who got charity from the lodges and under what circumstances brings us closer to knowing how people could live in a world where, in fact, merit counted for little, yet where people believed that it did, or at the least, that it should determine one's place or reward in society. Finally, chapter 5 turns to the volatile issue of what the lodges did about women, particularly in France, where their membership was significant and can be documented. We will see that the actual records from eighteenth-century lodges, as opposed to the inherited myths, can be quite revealing all by themselves.

CHAPTER 1

Origins

In 1717, four old London lodges consolidated and a remarkable social organization emerged. They formed the Grand Lodge of London, an umbrella organization to which other British, and eventually even foreign lodges would give their affiliation, and then as their numbers grew, seek to imitate. Within two decades Benjamin Franklin brought the freemasonry he had learned in London to Philadelphia. From this rather simple beginning grew an organization that by 1750 was steeped in controversy yet growing in popularity in both Europe and America.[1]

Who were these masons, why did they form a "Grand Lodge"? Were there no masons before 1717? Masons, carpenters, bakers, bell makers, barber-surgeons had all been protected and supervised by guilds for centuries in many European countries. Medieval and early modern guilds provided social life, benefits, wage protection, and quality control over skills and finished goods.[2] The identity of members and hence their right to work in places far from home was protected by secret words and handshakes. A worker who knew them was truly a member of the guide. Frequently, the guild masters acted in concert with town officials to maintain order and to ensure the stability of prices and wages as well as the quality of work.[3] But of the many medieval artisan crafts, only the masons' guilds survived the transition into modern market conditions by becoming something other than a protective and disciplining club for workers, by becoming freemasonry. [4]

In seventeenth-century urban Scotland and England, where the open, unprotected wage economy had become far advanced relative to the rest of Europe, lodges saw their numbers dwindle. They began to admit nonmasons largely because their dues were needed. The guild system had essentially broken down, and if buildings were to be built, capital was needed. What began out of necessity transformed this one guild into a voluntary society; in the process few of the original stonemasons found a place. Thus began a transformation that is sometimes called the transition from operative to speculative masonry; let us just call it the transition from masonic guild to freemasonry. The four London lodges must have gone through such a process. We meet them only in 1717 when the existence of the Grand Lodge became known. But the great English architect, Sir Christopher Wren, had been asked to head the London lodges as early as 1710—one of the few pieces of information we have about them before 1717.[5]

Besides conviviality and fellowship, the masonic lodges held other cultural attractions for merchants and gentlemen. Master masons were literate and known for their mathematical and architectural skills, particularly with fortifications, military and urban. The myth and lore associated with the lodges tied the geometrical skills of the masters with ancient learning supposedly inherited from the legendary Egyptian priest, Hermes Trismegistes.[6] He was thought to have taught Moses and to have transmitted a mystical understanding of the heavens that included a dedication to mathematics. Educated nonmasons may have been attracted to the lodges because of orally transmitted legends about their antiquity, and because in them the prosperous found useful men skilled in architecture and engineering. The mystical, in the form of the Hermetic tradition, combined with the utilitarian to bond brothers who became increasingly interested in the first, while shedding the second.[7]

Two individuals stand out from the transitional period of masonry as practiced by simple stone workers, to masonry as a new form of social fraternizing. One of the earliest nonmasons to be admitted into a lodge in the 1650s was Sir Robert Moray, a Scot, a man of the new science associated with Bacon and Descartes, and a military engineer.

He was also one of the founders of the Royal Society of London and a key player in the English civil wars. Moray, like the Oxford antiquarian, Elias Ashmole, who also accepted membership in a lodge in that decade, may have believed that masonry put him closer to the oldest tradition of ancient wisdom, associated with Hermes, out of which mathematics and the mechanical arts were said to have been nourished. Moray always signed his letters with his masonic emblem—a mark of his dedication to the ancient craft. For his part, Ashmole dabbled in alchemy (as did his contemporary Sir Isaac Newton) and may be described as a seeker after ancient lore and wisdom.[8] By the 1690s more and more gentlemen like Moray and Ashmole, some merchants, and others who were denizens of London political life had been brought into the lodges.

The details of the historical process by which, after 1650, a guild of workers evolved into a voluntary society of gentlemen are probably forever lost. While there are Scottish records, the English ones have mostly disappeared. As we will see with greater detail in Chapter 4, one lodge in Dundee, Scotland, shows nonmasons being admitted throughout the seventeenth century, but by 1700 the gentlemen have taken charge of the lodge.[9] The Scottish historian, David Stevenson, sees Scotland as the home of modern freemasonry.[10] It was—since lodges there were the first to become social clubs for the genteel. But the freemasonry of the eighteenth-century Enlightenment—the fraternity, ideals and constitution exported to continental Europe—encoded not the local Scottish customs and clan governance, but the institutions and constitutional ideals originating in the English Revolution against royal absolutism.

A manuscript from 1659, now housed in the Royal Society of London, makes the link between ancient wisdom and national governance. "This Craft . . . founded by worthy Kings and Princes and many other worshipful men" prescribes dedication to the seven liberal arts, particularly geometry. Hermes taught it and he was "the father of Wisemen [who] found out the two pillars of Stone whereon the Sciences were written and taught them forth, and at the making of the Tower of Babylon there was the craft of masonry found. . . ."[11] The manuscript narration about "Free Masons' Word and Signs," gives away its contemporary milieu, the revolution of the 1640s, the birth of constitutional government bound by laws or rules. It speaks in passing about "parliament" and further admonishes its members: "You shall . . . truly observe the Charges in the Constitution." It also invokes the ancient teacher and philosopher Hermes and the sciences that he taught. As we shall see in chapter 3, the document had been collected by the new Royal Society because it was attempting to write a history of all the trades and crafts—a project it never completed.

As the *Oxford English Dictionary* shows, the use of the term "constitution" to mean "rules, statutes, or charges" adopted by a body has few if any precedents prior to the 1650s. In that revolutionary decade, after the execution of Charles I in 1649, parliament enacted laws for the new republic. Simultaneously, voluntary societies with constitutions, however loosely structured, came into existence. At one point the 1659 document speaks quaintly of a French king as having been "elected," at another it speaks of a biblical time when "the King . . . made a great Councell and parliament was called to know how they might find meanes" to provide for the unemployed.[12] The English masons saw their history as inextricably bound up, not always happily, with the fate of kings and states. After 1700 they also came increasingly to be associated with a new cultural movement in favor of religious toleration and the end of censorship, the Enlightenment. Where we find the word "constitutions" being used in French for the first time to denote the rules or statutes of an organization (in 1710) the context is masonic and employs terms like "brothers" and "Grand Master."[13]

Of the many forms of new social behavior to become an integral part of enlightened culture during the eighteenth century, freemasonry has been the most difficult to understand. Secretive, ritualistic, devoted in many Grand Lodges to hierarchy—that would be one set of characteristics! But the eighteenth-century lodges also consistently spoke about civic virtue and merit, about men meeting as equals, about the need for brothers to become philosophers, about their being "enlightened." They said it in every European language: brothers must become in French *éclairé*, in Dutch *verlichte*, in German *aufgeklärt*.[14] Such lofty ideals surfaced early in the transition from masonic guild to the society of freemasons. With ideals and myths went a set of ancient practices and beliefs born in the guilds, but capable of being given modern meaning. By late in the century the egalitarian logic had spread—particularly in France—where, as shall see in the last chapter, women flocked to the new "lodges of adoption."

Now seen to be enlightened, masonic practices such as elections, majority rule, orations by elected officials, national governance under a Grand Lodge, and constitutions—all predicated on an ideology of equality and merit—owed their origin to the growth of parliamentary power, to the self-confidence of British urban merchants and landed gentry, and not least, to a literature of republican idealism. John Toland, a major republican Whig activist of the early eighteenth century, and his patron the Lord Mayor of London, Sir Robert Clayton, can be linked directly to London lodges that may have formed the nucleus of the Grand Lodge.[15] The masonic ideology of rising by merit, which justified egalitarian fraternizing among men of property free to chose their governors, belonged first and foremost to the English republican tradition. This identity did not prevent the lodges from being hierarchical and everywhere eager for aristocratic patronage, but it did ultimately tilt the lodges in the direction of being schools for government—more, rather than less, democratic government.

Such practices when taken onto the European Continent played into the love of secrecy found in court culture and imitated by elites, but in the new lodges secrecy and clubbing also inspired new degrees and ceremonies, and new political aspirations. By the later part of the century imitations of freemasonry appeared: such were the radical Illuminati founded in Bavaria in 1776.[16] They were an overtly political group, eager to reform German society. In general, whether in Europe or

America, masonic lodges sought never to be overtly political, never to take sides publicly. But the format of the lodge offered a template that other groups could imitate or embrace; it also offered men and some women the chance to imagine that they governed themselves competently.

The 1720s in London were critically important. The decade spawned the earliest lodges of literate gentlemen where few, if any, working stonemasons can be found. The evidence before 1717 shows lodges of gentlemen in London by the 1690s. Somewhere before 1717 the great architect, Sir Christopher Wren, presided as Grand Master, and the Grand Lodge took shape. By the 1730s the engraved picture that celebrated the lodges, and came from a Dutch source, had over one hundred meeting in pubs and claimed Sir Richard Steele, the great journalist of the period, as their guiding spirit.[17]

Sometime between the 1690s and 1723, when the Grand Lodge of London published its soon to be famous and often translated, *Constitutions*, the lodges became ever more fashionable.[18] The use of the plural, rather than the singular "constitution" in the 1723 document revealed it as an amalgam of various constitutions used by individual lodges. The term was unmistakably English. At this time in French, *une constitution* denoted the fact that a thing, like the human body, or eventually the government of a country, is composed of its constituent parts. The body's constitution is merely the sum of its organs and limbs, healthy or diseased. Only gradually in eighteenth-century French did the term come to denote rules and statutes, or an activity, as in a law not being constitutional and hence useless, or as in government by contract made by men who give it a constitution. That usage appears in a French book about the English "revolution" published in 1719.[19] As early as the first decade of the century, by contrast, the Grand Lodge of London was being constituted and governed by its brothers who have become very secular indeed.

The secular, even outrageously nonreligious side of freemasonry appeared very early in its history. The papers of John Toland now preserved in the British Library tell the story. He kept one meeting record of a group living in The Hague (where he was at the time), and, although written in French by men who had never been to England, the meeting used masonic words and phrases. They called one another "brother," they had a Grand Master, and constitutions, and they practiced secrecy.[20]

Thus in one of the early French documents from the new century that describes a voluntary society, we find a libertine and masonic group that met under their statutes or *constitutions*. The libertinism appears in the list of food and drink, and in the noticeable deterioration of the handwriting as the meeting proceeds. Associates of this group, among them a man who would become the leader of Amsterdam freemasonry, Jean Rousset de Missy, put into circulation the most outrageous document of a century filled with heresy. It argued that Jesus, Moses and Mohammed had been the three great imposters.[21] Even Voltaire was horrified by it when he read it.

Not surprisingly, the club, or society in The Hague, or as they called themselves, the order was composed not of English visitors, but of French Huguenot booksellers, journalists, publishers and probably one or two local men of science.[22] Many of its signatories were associates of the secretary of the group, the French refugee, Prosper Marchand. This French Protestant journalist, whose manuscripts are now housed at the University Library in Leiden, left behind one of the most important sources of information about early Continental freemasonry. He, or his friends, knew Toland who had traveled extensively on the Continent. Marchand and Rousset de Missy corresponded as close personal friends right up to Marchand's death in 1756. His last will and testament shows a palsied hand that wrote about religious ceremonies as "vain and contemptible."[23] A lodge could appeal to the uprooted, the mercantile, and the cosmopolitan, or the heretical: it was of ancient origin, democratic in its ethos, associated with the most advanced form of government to be found in Europe, and capable of being molded to one's tastes while offering charity and assistance to all brothers.

The group in The Hague used masonic terms like "Grand Master" while basically devoting themselves to eating and drinking. Yet among Marchand's closest friends, Rousset de Missy, another refugee, led Amsterdam freemasonry and became a political agent first for the House of Orange and then for the Austrians. His lifelong passion included a hatred of French absolutism, while in religion he privately described himself as a "pantheist."[24] The word had been invented by Toland to describe his personal creed.[25] Rousset passionately loved his lodge in Amsterdam and wanted it to be a place where virtue and probity, tied to no religion, could be cultivated.

A mason of any lodge had to be "of the religion of that country or nation whatever it was," but the 1723 *Constitutions* said that "tis now thought more expedient only to oblige [the freemason] to that religion in which all men agree."[26] In deference to the deep religious divisions in Britain, freemasonry endorsed a minimalist creed which could be anything from theism to pantheism and atheism. Not surprisingly, the lodges in England had a high representation of Whigs and scientists, while in Paris at mid-century the freemason Helvétius was a materialist and in Amsterdam, Rousset de Missy was a pantheist. The great political theorist, Montesquieu, also a freemason, was probably some kind of deist. In both London and Amsterdam Jewish names can be found in the lodge records. In France there were lodges for both Protestants and Catholics, indeed even actors, often scorned in polite society, were admitted. In one Paris lodge letters between brothers mention a "Negro trumpeter" in the King's regimen.[27] Rarely do lodge ceremonies, even in Catholic countries, contain overtly Christian language.

When the Catholic Church condemned lodge membership in 1738 it objected that freemasonry constituted a new form of religion. It also condemned frequent elections as being republican.[28] For some men freemasonry expressed new beliefs that were tolerant and endorsed practices ultimately at odds with traditional religiosity and monarchical absolutism. The Church's condemnation only made the lodges more attractive to the secular-minded and the progressive. It is hardly surprising that by 1750 membership in a masonic lodge had come to denote enthusiasm for the new, enlightened ideas, although not necessarily for the materialism and atheism associated with some of the *philosophes*.

Thanks to the records that came back from Moscow only in 2000, the evidence is now clear that in the 1740s in France women also belonged to lodges. A note on the bottom of one record mentions the local women's lodge in Bordeaux. In The Hague in 1751 a lodge of men and women used French as its first language and left a list of its officers in both the masculine and the feminine, *Le Maitre*, *La Maitresse*, and so on. Local actors and actresses in the Comédie française housed in the town fraternized with nobleman and wealthy merchants.[29] They were even attacked for doing so by a local abbé. Traditionally we see eighteenth-century women as less attracted to the heresies associated with the Enlightenment than men. But the masonic ceremonies we can trace to them suggest an ability to be just as secular as their brothers. We will learn more about these women in Chapter five.

But the lodges were about more than social and intellectual life. The self-governance of lay elites outside of confraternities or town councils, and operating in local groups joined on a national scale, was rare in continental Europe during the eighteenth century. Within the masonic lodges as they spread first to the Dutch Republic and France, then as far east as Prague and Moscow, and as far west as Philadelphia and Cap Français (Haiti), secular-minded, affluent men, and some women, began governing themselves: in colonial settings as part of their empires, at home as part of their localities and through the Grand Lodges, their nations. Lodge membership became a symbol of independence from clerical authority and a sign of political maturity. It also became one means of insuring cultural cohesion among Europeans in their colonies, an expression of imperial status just like that offered by the churches and scientific societies.

Government ministers, state employees, liberal professionals like lawyers, doctors and teachers, as well as merchants, flocked to join the lodges. In Sweden the entire court from the king and his ministers on down joined lodges that were feted at the royal palace.[30] There, as in Britain and the American colonies, the lodges paraded in public, a sign of their acceptance. In Paris and The Hague British ambassadors played a role in spreading the fraternity. We know about the French connection because in the 1730s the police raided the Paris home of the British ambassador, Lord Waldegrave, in part because a lodge was meeting there.[31] In Berlin by 1750 Frederick the Great used the lodges to enhance his own cultlike following. In Vienna in the 1780s Joseph II's influence permeated the lodges where Mozart sought out his musical commissions.

Everywhere they spread, the lodges also denoted relative affluence, drinking, and merrymaking. Despite their conspicuous consumption, the lodges were also places that sought to instill decorum, at least before dinner. Modifying the behavior of men helped to internalize discipline and manners. In London lodges would sometimes take over the theater for a performance, and there is evidence that brothers behaved better than audiences did typically. The habits of listening and silence in theaters and concerts developed only slowly, largely by the second half of the eighteenth century and as part of a general growth of decorum, politeness, and interiority. The masonic lodges played a role in that self-disciplining process. The Enlightenment needs to be seen as a complex mix of new ideas as well as habits: public discussion, sociability, private, uncensored reading. All required a new, more commonplace sense of an inner self that took pride in discipline and decorum. Lodges, like other forms of sociability, helped to instill it.

In every European country masonic dues were substantial (although graded by ability to pay), and each lodge came to possess a social persona and to give loyalty to a national Grand Lodge. Some lodges spurned anyone but the noble-born; others were entirely for students or doctors. Some lodges admitted lowly merchants, even actors; others banned them. Dues varied according to the means of the brothers and the relationship between the lodge and a brother was partly contractual, based upon dues paid, and partly filial.

In the 1780s, when the French Grand Lodge was dispensing charity to brothers, widows, and aged women freemasons, their letters tell much about being caught between two worlds: one modern and based upon contract, the other essentially feudal and based upon birth and deference. As we will see in greater detail in chapter 4, in the same letter freemasons could beg and supplicate while noting that in their youth or wealth they had paid their dues, feted their brothers, and been good citizens in their respective lodges. They were owed assistance, they implied, yet they knew that it had to come from the aristocratic leadership of the Grand Lodge—hence they pleaded.

Lodge membership could begin to resemble citizenship in a state, a presumed right to participate or even to govern. We can see this forward-looking aspect of lodge membership most clearly in the Austrian case. In the very Catholic Austrian territories after 1750 lodge membership signaled support for enlightened reform against the traditional privileges of the clergy. Men in the secular professions were drawn into such lodges. By the 1780s the Grand Lodge in Vienna worked with the government, in one instance to suppress lodges in the restless western colony of the southern Netherlands, Belgium. The Viennese Grand Lodge authorized only three lodges, closed down all others and drew up lists of appropriate members. In July 1786 the Vienna lodge proudly informed Joseph II that "the General Government of masonry is now in conformity with your edicts."[32] As we shall see in greater detail in Chapter 3, on this occasion a fraternal organization, commonplace in European civil society, assisted the state in remaking the contours of another colonial society under its jurisdiction.

The masonic instinct for governance fueled identification with the center, with national institutions. In 1756 when Dutch freemasons organized their national system of authority and governance, the Grand Lodge of the Netherlands, they adopted "the form" of the Estates General of the Republic. Furthermore they recommended it to German lodges that were having difficulty arriving at a comparable system of national cohesion. An Estates General, the Dutch said, could work as "the sovereign tribunal of the Nation."[33] They meant the masonic nation. Just like the Estates General where each province retained a high degree of sovereignty, in the Dutch lodges decentralized governance permitted independence. In the 1750s the Grand Master in The Hague, the Baron de Boetzelaer, spoke about the freemasons holding a "national assembly" there. At these assemblies the ceremonies placed brothers standing in rows, the first row symbolizing the "Staten van Holland," the legislative body of the province of Holland.[34] After a detailed symbolic arrangement, they affirmed national unity. By the 1750s nationalism was rising throughout western Europe, possibly aided by masonic practices.

Identity with the nation did not inhibit masonic cosmopolitanism. We see it in every major city where lodges might have regular visitors from anywhere in the Western world and its colonies, correspond likewise throughout the world, and yet, simultaneously, see the nation as a site where virtue and merit should be rewarded. In the early 1780s the lodge in Amsterdam entertained a brother from Philadelphia.[35] We may easily imagine that the American Revolution, which the Dutch had partly financed, was high on the list of topics under discussion. The Enlightenment initiated reforming impulses that were felt in many areas, but its assault on privilege and corruption also suggested to secular-minded elites that new men were needed in government service. More than any other new form of sociability, the lodges became schools of government, places where the reformist impulses of the Enlightenment could be focused on one's immediate surroundings, potentially on one's immediate province or state. They were also places where brothers could hear a firsthand account of revolutions on distant shores as models for their own revolutions. In the late 1780s these broke out in Amsterdam and Brussels, most spectacularly in Paris.

The masonic gestures imitative of national government can also be seen in the records of French freemasonry. In 1738 in Paris a Jacobite refugee from Scotland, the Chevalier Ramsay, gave what became a famous oration, in which he said that freemasonry attempts to create "an entire spiritual nation." Copies of the oration turn up in Reims, Dijon, and The Hague. In the 1760's a piece of French masonic jewelry, confiscated from its Jewish engraver by the authorities in Brussels, displayed "the arms of France illuminating the attributes of freemasonry."[36] By the 1770s the unified French lodges were focused on the institutions of central authority, beginning with a revitalized Grand Lodge.

In 1774 the new Grand Lodge of Paris chose to establish a national assembly. Representatives came from all over the country and each had one vote.[37] All were expected to pay taxes to the Grand Lodge. At the time of the first national assembly, no such institution existed in France. If a man or a woman was a freemason, might the conclusion be that masonic government was superior to what existed in France? In 1779 an orator in Grenoble lamented that "in our modern institutions where the form of government is such that the majority of subjects must stay in the place assigned them by nature, how is it possible to contribute to the common good?"[38] In the 1770s the French Grand Lodge sought to contribute to the common good by having a public presence in Paris. The relationship between the French lodges and the state had gotten off to a bad start when, in the early 1740s, the chief minister of state, Cardinal Fleury, had them spied upon. By the 1770s the Grand Lodge presented a public face of absolute loyalty to church and crown. But ordinary brothers had begun to resent the sycophantic aristocrats who controlled it.

In addition to a national representative assembly with one man, one vote, the Grand Lodge set up charity funds for brothers and sisters fallen on hard times. Seeing oneself as capable of constituting the polity and tending to its needs made freemasons into a new breed of political men—not necessarily disloyal or even republican—but with a new, and potentially dangerous, confidence about self-governance. In the case of charity they even supplanted the government in an age when governmental welfare was unknown. The freemasons did not cause the French Revolution of 1789, as the conspiracy theorists right up to the Nazis claimed, but they did make it more rather than less likely to happen.

The same impulse to govern surfaced in the women's lodges which spread rapidly on the Continent. In them women could identify themselves as enlightened, worship the God of Newtonian science, the Grand Architect, as He was called by the freemasons, invent rituals, and give orations. In one women's ritual the principal figure was the Queen of the Amazons. She ran the ceremonies, despite the 1723 *Constitutions*, which had said that women could not even join lodges. The Queen initiated both men and women and her female officers had military titles. The catechism of the lodge called on women to recognize the injustice of men and to throw off the masculine yoke, to dominate in marriage and to claim equal wealth with men. In one ceremony the Queen holds the constitutions and queries the "Grand Patriarch:" How do men keep women under them? She then urges her sisters to cast off the bondage imposed by men, to regard as tyrants those who will not obey women.[39] By the 1780s the lodges in France had become focuses for innovation, particularly in the area of relations between men and women.

Freemasonry could make abstract ideals like reason, equality, and self-governance concrete, even if difficult to attain. By 1750 around fifty thousand European and American men had joined lodges; by 1785 there were probably well over fifteen hundred women freemasons. The colonial numbers are unknown, but the lodges, like the churches, spread with empire. They expressed the highest ideals articulated during the age of Enlightenment; they could also be places of exclusion, purposefully remote from peasants, workers, in many places women, and in all places slaves. Yet in their search for equality and merit, for self-governance, free speech and religious toleration, the lodges look to the future, toward human rights and egalitarian ideals. For that reason alone they would be hated by the enemies of democracy, both in the eighteenth century and also in some of the recently created emerging eastern European and Russian democracies. It is still possible to get into a taxi in Moscow and be told that the country is being run by Jews and freemasons.

Many of these aspects of eighteenth-century freemasonry are explored in the pages ahead. We will examine the role of governance in the lodges and the symbiotic relationship between civil society and the growing power of the state. We will also look at the masonic charity funds that operated in France during the 1780s and examine the tensions they reveal in a society soon to be convulsed by revolution. Women's freemasonry also receives attention; it is a subject too long neglected in books about freemasonry. But before these specific topics can be broached, we need to know something about the daily lives and ideals of the fraternity.

In the next chapter I try to give a sense of what daily life may have been like for brothers and sisters. We have a superb collection of pocket diaries or almanacs, largely from the Library of the Grand Lodge in The Hague, which tell us a great deal about what the user may have thought as he or she recorded tasks or appointments; checked for the times of coaches; and in rare moments of leisure, read the almanac with its masonic orations, engraved ceremonies, and moral admonitions. For its true believers freemasonry was meant to be lived, not simply joined. The most startling aspect of masonic day-to-day living lay in the penchant of the lodges to invent forms of governance. These began with dues and oaths of loyalty, but then extended to behavior that suggests citizenship: voting, orating before one's brothers, setting the terms of officers and elections, and offering prescriptions for civic life within the lodge, even policing mores. Such habits have become harmless enough, but in the eighteenth century governance everywhere was the designated work of kings, churches, or elites. Blood and ordination counted in matters of government, but in the lodges—it was claimed—merit and discipline determined status. Perhaps it was inevitable that the enemies of democracy would come late in the century to blame the freemasons for its revolutionary manifestations.

CHAPTER 2

Daily Lives as Measured in Masonic Time

Getting at the daily rhythms or thoughts of people in the past presents a challenge. Today our lives would appear in outline in our daily diaries, written or electronic. Trips to the doctor mix with important events in personal and family life, also with information deemed necessary for daily living: phone numbers, holidays, days when the government closes and so on. Framed in day-to-day time we jot our lives down, almost in passing, perhaps never imagining that hundreds of years from now our pocket diaries might prove to be very interesting. Such daily jottings from the eighteenth century are rare, almost nonexistent. But we do possess multiple copies of the small, printed books, generally called almanacs, that people used to get at the information they needed, like the times of coaches, or about how to get around in a city, find the right merchant or court, or to look up the day of the week on which Christmas would fall. Seeing a specific market, publishers made such almanacs for freemasons. The way they record time, and provide readings to assist in its passage, especially concerns us.

We would give the world to know how such an eighteenth-century diary was used, how personal events mixed with the printed outline of the year around which it would be lived. We would love to know whether women used their daily diaries differently from men; perhaps they took fewer coaches but needed to know the days of holidays more exactly. The information about actual use is probably lost forever. Neither in masonic nor in general pocket diaries—both often described as

FIGURE 4. Frontispiece to *De Almanach der Vrye Metzelaaren . . . 1780* (Amsterdam: Willem Coertze, Jr.), showing a woman holding a square and compasses. The use of women as allegorical figures was commonplace in masonic symbolism of the age. With permission of the masonic library, Prins Frederik Cultural Masonic Center, The Hague; copyright Grand East of the Netherlands.

almanacs—do handwritten jottings appear with any frequency. Most times we have no idea who owned the diary, or even if particular copies preserved in libraries throughout Europe or America were anything more than part of a print overrun, just one copy that never got sold.

We can extrapolate from the printed contents of pocket almanacs as to what their publishers—especially when many of them were freemasons—thought would best sell the diaries or almanacs to a consumer. Masonic almanacs interest us most compellingly in this chapter, but they are best seen in light shone by general almanacs intended for any literate reader. One remarkable feature stands out that separates most masonic diaries from those aimed at a general audience. Most general diaries contained pious sentiments that invoked religious pieties and Godly thoughts. Not the masonic ones. In large measure their publishers cast the contents of diaries aimed at the fraternity in decidedly secular terms. It seems reasonable to suggest that publishers probably knew their audiences.

Before we dwell upon the striking differences between masonic almanacs and ones aimed at the general public, some similarities are worth noting. At first, masonic and other diaries were hardly pocket-size, but by mid-century they began to resemble what we routinely carry with us today. They were light-weight, small, and hence fragile. Generally, eighteenth-century owners put their names in a diary's margin, just as they occasionally recorded in cramped spaces important birth and death dates. Sometimes a personal note slipped through. Take an American entry that vividly reminds us of a lost world. An almanac jotting in a margin from one month in 1729 tells us that "Black Nanny died the 20th day."[1] But she is as unknowable as are most of the owners of pocket almanacs, masonic or non, slave-owning or not. In the paucity of available blank pages and in the absence of detailed jottings, eighteenth-century almanacs, generic or masonic, differ from our diaries, which first and foremost provide real space for a listing of our personal affairs. People in the eighteenth century must have kept such diurnal agendas in their heads, or put them in the traditional personal, sometimes confessional or spiritual diaries.[2] Those, however, generally recorded events after they happened.

We have few such poignant entries in European almanacs, masonic or otherwise, as the one about the death of an American slave nanny. Samples from the print runs of these small, fragile books nonetheless survive—to be found in multiple editions—because so many businessmen and travelers needed them. They were deeply utilitarian in purpose, yet interspersed with a wide variety of thoughts, aphorisms and pieties. Thus both general and masonic diaries give us glimpses, however nearly opaque, into the daily thoughts available to their users. The almanacs provided information about everything from coach times to the meeting hours of local courts and, in the case of diaries made for freemasons, the location of lodges in multiple cities. Eighteenth-century almanacs, whether masonic or generic, were meant to be predictive and reliable guides to the world at a glance. As a genre the almanac stretched well back into the early seventeenth century, but it came into its own, and into a mass circulation, largely in the eighteenth.[3]

We focus on the diaries bought by freemasons and published especially for their use. The diaries allow us to inch our way closer to the lives of their masonic users, without letting us assume that the buyer subscribed to all the sentiments found in a diary. Perhaps inevitably, by the 1730s enterprising publishers saw the masonic market for such diaries and began to produce them with a style and content that they thought would sell. The repetition of themes and ideas suggest that by the mid-eighteenth century masonic formulas had emerged that were commercially successful enough to warrant repetition. Indeed, aside from farmers, freemasons were among the few groups whom publishers sought specifically to woo, and decade by decade masonic almanacs—as far as we can tell from what survives in libraries—became more numerous. The genre began in 1735 when William Smith, a London publisher, produced the first masonic "pocket companion," as he called it.[4]

Alas, not as many masonic pocket companions from Britain and America have survived as we would like. The best examples of such almanacs come from the Dutch Republic: there are boxes of them housed with meticulous care at the Library of the Grand East in The Hague. They could be in Dutch or French, since the latter language was used by many in the republic. Also with a French text the publisher had a larger, international audience. We can imagine such a diary selling in Belgium, Switzerland, France, or even Germany where the educated often used French.

Mostly the masonic diaries found today in The Hague will provide our examples, bearing in mind that the ones in Dutch, like their British counterparts, were aimed at a largely Protestant audience. We would expect Catholics to be more wrapped in the daily liturgy of the saints in part because Protestants had frowned upon their cults, relics, and statues. Predictably the French diaries offered a diurnal religiosity and gave every day its proper saint. Neither religion had the edge, however, when it came to piety or a sense of the afterlife, the religious time-out-of-mind that promised salvation and that was plainly visible in the almanacs aimed at the larger public.

Being involved in this secular world, hence the need for such a practical diary, could be seen by both Catholics and Protestants as a distraction from Godliness. This fear of worldliness may account for the overall pious tone adopted by generic diary after diary. After a user managed to catch the coach listed in an almanac, the time could be passed by the reading of pious texts. Thus the appearance of secular themes, and the general absence of a specified religion in masonic diaries—as seen in every European language—becomes distinctive. Such worldliness strikes the historian as particularly interesting. So too in the masonic diaries a remarkable cosmopolitanism surfaces and complements their generally secular stance. Seldom did a masonic diary fail to mention the locations of lodges in other countries, or events of importance wherever freemasons had an interest. A German masonic diary sang the praises of the local rulers and the protection they gave the lodges. Nary a religious theme appears; only the unity of the freemasons mattered.[5]

Most nonmasonic diaries never cast their geographical gaze so far and wide. Some generic American ones, even in the years of the French Revolution, made no reference to events in Europe.[6] Others did at least give an estimate of the population of the various European countries.[7] But the English language diaries from both Britain and the American colonies did lay emphasis upon the chronology of the monarchy and who sat on the British throne at the moment. Whether general or masonic, diaries inculcated the broad outlines of royal government and dynastic succession. They achieved a timelessness, or regularity, as sure as the phases of the moon or the setting of the winter sun.

One of the earliest American masonic diaries appears aimed at both a generic and a masonic audience; perhaps we have in it evidence of a publisher who hedged his bets. This early American diary also possessed distinctively American qualities. In contrast to the European diaries for freemasons, the American one gave an eccentric history of the origins of the order, one that laid emphasis upon the working men in the earliest lodges. In English, French, and Dutch language diaries the story of the origins of the fraternity stuck pretty close to the account given in Anderson's *Constitutions* of 1723. It laid emphasis upon royal patronage and architects as the key to masonic evolution. We know, however, from the work of Steven Bullock that in the American colonies by the 1760s the lodges had become "ancient" and had broken with the orthodoxy of the Grand Lodge and its official history. The early American diary of 1764 bowed briefly in the direct of royal patronage for the order. Then, with a feisty tone, it said that the stonemasons, patronized by Edward III, "agreed upon Tokens etc. to know one another by, and to assist one another against being impressed and not to work unless *free*, and on their own terms"; hence they were called freemasons. It even said that the fraternity in those olden days enjoyed equality with the royal Order of the Garter.[8] It was artisans and not architects who inspired the American masonic imagination, both white and black.[9]

All these sentiments suggest that by the 1760s in the colonies a high degree of independence from the imperial or royal narrative of freemasonry had come to prevail. As Steven Bullock shows, such independence of spirit had become symptomatic of a larger movement stirring among the general American population. The rest of this early American diary, aimed only in part at a masonic audience, is relatively unremarkable except, just as we shall see with its European counterparts that it gave an entirely secular chronology of important dates from Roman times onward. It also added some astrology, an essay on health by the famous English doctor George Cheyne, a list of all the English kings, and a curious essays on love and marriage, supposedly by the seventeenth-century English scientist Robert Boyle. In it we learn of his sentiment "I have seldom seen a happy marriage." One might contemplate that grim thought while on a stage wagon, picked up conveniently because the times and prices were given in the diary.

An American masonic diary from just into the new century, 1801, suggests that the secularism of the eighteenth century was distinctive to the colonial age that spawned Franklin and Jefferson. In the first year of the nineteenth century the pocket almanac gives saints' days as well as all the secular dates, the Fourth of July for example, and provides an extensive list of lodges all over the new republic and even in Port-au-Prince, Haiti. All the officers of the Philadelphia lodges are listed. But a closing poem points to a renewal of religious sentiment, "Let us also inwardly digest the holy bible; let its doctrines & precepts even accompany our conditions in life that we may, like true Masons, dwell even here in the house of the Lord our God, and admire the beauties of his holy temple." Uncharacteristically for an earlier age, brothers are then admonished to have faith in Christ.[10] Yet a slightly later masonic almanac, for 1814, has songs and gives heads of government in Pennsylvania and is devoid of religious overtones.[11] We know nothing about the religiosity of the owners of these almanacs intended for a pocket. They might have been pious or not; we are just lucky to have them at all.

Except for their preservation, these small, commonplace American or European items, pocket diaries or almanacs, would be unremarkable save for the noticeable difference between eighteenth-century masonic ones and those meant for a general audience. In the age of Enlightenment, freemasons on both sides of the Atlantic seemed more comfortable in this world's time, without seeing the need of being reminded about eternal time. Some masonic diaries gave the saints' days, even the date of the creation of the world, for example, 5742, and the year of the flood, 4686—all earnestly offered. Christian dating was also commonplace in diaries aimed at a general audience.[12] Of course, the year for the building of the Temple of Solomon (2810), said in masonic mythology to have been the work of the fraternity, would be a natural piece of masonic chronology, and one date not found in generic diaries.[13] But by and large, other important pieties were missing from pocket diaries aimed at a masonic audience. Whether in English, French, or Dutch, talk about how "the great God of nature forewarns a sinful world of approaching calamities," or about the laws of nature revealing the majesty of God, is strangely absent from the masonic repertoire.[14] Some diaries for the general public on occasion broke with the generally naturalist reading of comets and insisted upon seeing them "as God's Hand, and take Notice of the divine Pleasure and Design in them."[15] By contrast, masonic diaries waxed eloquent with vagaries, more secular than religious, "to adore a supreme Being is always the first principle of our Ancestors . . . a mason consecrates the premises of his work to the Eternal . . . he is equally remote from ridiculous incredulity and superstitious fanaticism."[16] A masonic poem found in one French diary put its religious sensibility nicely: "In Religion and in Politics [la Politique] / We never neglect la Pratique."[17]

Overwhelmingly all diaries betrayed their origins in the new scientific culture. Invariably their authors or compilers described themselves as astronomers, natural philosophers, or mathematicians. One British almanac writer said he was "Philomath."[18] Occasionally a diary might be done by "a student in physick and astrology."[19] Such a diary might assert "the government of the Moon over the body of man, as she passeth the 12 zodiacal constellations."[20] Yet even when tilting toward astrology, every diary taught basic astronomy and gave naturalistic explanations for comets or eclipses. But when aimed at the general market, as distinct from a masonic one, the almanacs largely kept to a pious theme. The age called that particular mix physico-theology, and generic almanacs loved to invoke it. Boston almanacs told users of 1762 that, as they ventured in the British empire, "Ye Christians as their plenteous Wealth you share, / With your best faith enrich the Natives there."[21] American diaries, like British ones, invoked the pious poetry and prose of Pope, Dryden, Addison, and the ubiquitous Dr. Cheyne, who preached sound body and mind as the natural state to which Christians should strive. Some American diaries gave the meeting times of churches or Quaker groups. British diaries frequently gave the names of all the bishops, archbishops, and deans, and of course, listed the Anglican holy days. By mid-century, however, the pious genre was less common even in generic diaries. They might offer medical advice as well as giving high tides and the times for a full moon.[22] Sometimes mathematical exercises were offered, for both men and women.[23]

Without exception all diaries taught history and gave chronologies. Even if the masonic dates were a bit fanciful, the impulse found in many diaries, to order history and put the year in question in its chronological place, made a serious contribution to giving people a sense of historical development and change. The time being presented was often religious time, but just as important, and more frequently than in nonmasonic diaries of the period, masonic time could be measured in public events, battles, wars, the death of kings.[24] It might even be possible to pass the time using one's diary, masonic or not, to assist with memorizing a list of all the kings of France or England.

This secular quality to be found especially in masonic almanacs and diaries foreshadows much of our own sense of time as being historical. A sense of history as something unfolding in the here and now belongs distinctively to Western modernity. Historical time was invented in European consciousness in the seventeenth and eighteenth centuries.

In the diaries and almanacs such time became commonplace, available to any literate reader, masonic or not.

While the masonic diaries gave a sense of history, theirs could also often be a fanciful sense. One reason it has been so hard for us to sort out masonic facts from fictions has been masonry's eighteenth-century ancestors, who took up every imaginable story to make the lodges seem as old as Western civilization itself. Take this one from a masonic diary: "Upon the introduction of the Romans into Britain, arts and sciences began to flourish apace. In the progress of civilization, Masonry came into esteem, and was much encouraged by Caesar, and several of the Roman generals, who succeeded him in the government of this island."[25] Julius Caesar had protected the lodges! The problem with the story is that there is not a shred of historical evidence to support it. The tales continued: in 600 the archbishop of Canterbury "appeared at the head of the fraternity." Of course William the Conqueror also protected "the fraternity" and it in turn built the Tower of London, not to mention London Bridge and a host of other important buildings. As guild evolved into voluntary society the society of freemasons appropriated the guild history (indeed stonemasons built all those buildings; who else would have?). And then they added flourishes that still turn up in the twenty-first century. "During the reign of Henry II the grand master of the Knights Templars superintended the Masons, and employed them in building their Temple in Fleet Street, A.D. 1155."[26] Dan Brown could have gotten part of the fanciful chronology of his novel confirmed by that diary.

Some of this mythical history, of uncertain origin, had also been incorporated into the *Constitutions* of 1723, and that canonical text in turn went through a multitude of editions in just about every Western language. The 1723 book, so basic to freemasonry, went hand in hand with the masonic diaries of European origin. The *Constitutions* also had very little to say about religious belief, except to note that the freemason should be of what ever religion to which all men agree. It also gave a potted history of England with reference to which king or queen had done what to the freemasons.

The *Constitutions* said that freemasonry had not fared well in the reign of Elizabeth. The almanacs elaborated with the tale that the queen sent "an armed force to York, with intent to break up their annual communication." She thought that the freemasons were withholding secrets. The Grand Master disabused her of the notion and proclaimed the brothers to be "skillful architects, who cultivated arts and science another, and never meddled in affairs of church or state."[27] By the time the histories got to the late seventeenth century, they settled into more believable stories, or at least ones that historians can check against other sources. Sir Christopher Wren and Robert Clayton appeared as early founders of gentlemen's freemasonry.[28] Other documents from the period, or from private letters slightly later, suggest their involvement. Helpfully the diaries also listed all the national officers right up to the year in question.

In their fashion the diaries, whether masonic or aimed at a general audience, may also be seen as teaching devices. For example, sometimes they gave the order of the planets (and their signs), the eclipses of the sun; "following Copernicus, the earth and not the moon is a planet."[29] All taught the simplest astronomy, but occasionally even the masonic ones could allude to astrological themes.[30] Science and magic mixed freely with the dates for the beginning of Lent, Easter, the Ascension of Christ, and the start of Advent. The pattern of mixing the credulous with the scientific began earlier in the century and can be seen in almanacs now preserved in Anglo-American libraries.[31] In diaries that might have been aimed at both a Catholic and Protestant audience, the saints' days were also catalogued.

In the masonic diaries more was to be taught than the rhythm of the originally Christian calendar. Always they aimed to inculcate virtuous behavior. In order to distinguish a true brother from a false one the reader should observe that the first eschews "ambition, vain glory and interest," and he seeks truth par excellence, as well as the practice of charity. Always the true brothers are "children of the light"; and at the same time "the man who is morally free is truly free." Sometimes a vague religiosity is also invoked: "The heart is the foundation upon which the freemason builds, for the glorification of the supreme being, the Sovereign Architect of the Universe . . . it is necessary to police our mores, finally so that our actions will be able to be, like a cubed gem, an appropriate part of a mystical temple."[32] This fairly minimalist creed could be practiced by any earnest brother or sister. Funeral orations, often printed in the almanacs, brought home the this-worldly quality of masonic virtue. Heaven went unmentioned and the deceased brother won praise for having a "sensibility that united at its base humanity, sweetness, charity, that had given him a love of the poor for which all men would have been jealous."[33] At the masonic funeral for Voltaire, music and song celebrated "the great man" who had become "the founder of a New World." The brothers, V. F. de la Lande, the painter, Greuze, the visiting American, Benjamin Franklin, and sister Madame de Villete, laid wreaths at the foot of his statue.[34]

The universalism of the masonic message can be deduced from the extent of the territory an almanac imagined for its sales. More than a sense of local time and place appeared in masonic diaries aimed conceivably at the entire European market. Many diaries gave a list of lodges in every city and, remarkably, in the colonies of the Dutch Republic, or of France. Sometimes the date and place of meetings were offered.[35] Wherever the language used in the almanac was spoken lay a potential market, both at home and abroad. Perhaps membership in lodges overseas served as another way for the beneficiaries of the empire to feel "at home." Lodges, like churches and chapels, gave Europeans a sense of identity whether in Suriname or St. Dominque. They helped to unify the empire.

The sense of recognition and identity that lodges offered was only reenforced by the many attempts to apply uniformity to their proceedings. Rituals repeated, and similar from lodge to lodge, meant that brothers and sisters away from home could participate in the proceedings. Supposedly all these were secret, but the almanacs often reveal that masonic secrecy was honored more in the breech than in the execution. Some diaries had engravings that depicted masonic ceremonies, perhaps intended to make sure that they conformed to a pattern wherever they might be performed. We can imagine a brother in his coach en route to a lodge meeting frantically going over the details of an elaborate ceremony, memorizing where the master should stand or the new "secret" password to be given out that day and conveniently printed in the pocket almanac for that year. Some of the rituals described in the almanacs were elaborate and almost religious in their emotional tone, for example, rituals that imitated death and rebirth. They must have made a strong impression on the person being initiated, and perhaps these descriptions can help us better understand why the lodges for women asked that the initiate not be pregnant at the time.

Into the pocket of any brother also came knowledge of foreign dignitaries admitted to the masonic order. In London in 1777, brothers were told, the oldest son of the Nabab of Carnatica, Madras, became a freemason.[36] But the admission of indigenous peoples was on the whole rare. The lodges were for the imperialists. The entire globe, as surveyed and dominated by Westerners, became a part of daily consciousness. Lists provided the names of all Grand Lodges in North America, the Bahamas, Armenia, and Belgium, and they complemented extensive lists of European lodges. Triumphantly, alphabetical lists were given of "the principal lodges established in the four corners of the world."[37] So too lists appeared of all the kings in Europe who were members of the order, or just as important, its protectors.[38] We can imagine that the diaries were therefore also intended to serve travelers far from home and looking for fraternal company. Not surprisingly, coach times and prices were also printed.

Perhaps such lists suggest a certain dryness in the subject matter of masonic diaries, that the lists look like the string of 800 free phone numbers provided in many of our own diaries. But lodges in the eighteenth century, like the diaries intended for their members, also sought to instill orderliness, as well as to edify and sometimes to be polemical.

FIGURES 5–9. In *De Almanach der Vrye Metzelaaren . . . 1780* (Amsterdam) we find these elaborate ceremonies engraved for readers. The numbers correspond to the titles given in the text: 1 is the Grand Master, 2 is the speaker (for that meeting), and so on. The images show the candidate being received into the lodge (Figure 5) and being positioned to be received (Figures 6, 7); the ceremony complete with the laying on of swords (Figure 8); and the candidate, still blindfolded, being raised up by his new "brothers" (Figure 9). In effect he is being laid on the masonic carpet as if he were dead, to be "marked" by his brothers, given the secret password "Tubalkain," and finally "resurrected" into his new masonic life.

All those themes appear in the diaries. When a new lodge was opened in The Hague in 1761, the Equality of Brothers, the opening discourse in French appeared in a diary as late as 1793. Elsewhere I have argued that the lodge, and its name, may have been opened in reaction against the lodge for men and women that had flourished in the city at mid-century.[39] Reprinting the opening oration, again and again, may have been a way of continuing opposition to women being in the lodges. Perhaps the brothers who wanted to dwell solely on their equality had in their disapproving mind lodges of adoption, women's lodges in Bordeaux, or one closer to home in The Hague. Other diaries offered more gender-benign poems and songs, "A brother has a heart for the work/ He lives more content than a King."[40] The tune to which it was to be sung in French was also provided. Still other almanacs, in search of gender equality, gave ceremonies to be used by men and women at a masonic "fête de table." "We drink brothers, we drink to our amicable sisters," who in turn answered, "We drink to our tender *confrères*."[41]

In general, moral uplift, rather than gender polemics, filled the pages of typical diaries. "The lodges must be schools of the Moral and Philosophy . . . in effect . . . in the discourses that are spoken in them, always Virtue, Charity, and the Love of our neighbor, lie at the base of our intentions." So said a French diary published in The Hague in 1781.[42] It also published an oration given to the national Grand Lodge in The Hague the previous year. The speaker praised the Dutch nation and also asked the Grand Architect of the Universe "to perpetuate generation after generation a race of citizens useful to their country, heroic defenders of Liberty and Religion, and enlightened masters who can revivify our virtues."[43] The appearance of liberty in the language in that year suggests a number of possibilities. The reference may reflect the growing impact of the American Revolution in European consciousness. But the implication that virtue needs reviving may also signal the growing discontent seen in the Dutch Republic by the 1780s. By 1787 revolution would erupt in Amsterdam that was only put to rest by the invasion of Prussian soldiers. We can only wonder what loyal freemasons made of those events because this same diary was warm in its praise of Frederick, king of Prussia, who a mere seven years later ordered the antirevolutionary invasion. We know that some lodges supported the revolution, and that others were Orangist, supporting the stadtholder and the Prussians.

But overt politics seldom appear in the pages of the diaries, or in the orations given in lodges that we know from other sources. At moments the diaries were even prepared to do the bidding of monarchs, as in the diary of 1787 that published a decree from Joseph II of Austria that restricted the number of lodges permitted in Belgium.[44] As we shall see in the next chapter, the emperor had become suspicious of the multiple forms of civil society flourishing in his kingdom. In general masonic diaries erred on the side of political caution. Nothing in them matched the overtly revolutionary themes to be found in at least one almanac aimed at a general American audience. Clearly by or near 1775 the British authorities in the colony had lost the ability to censor, and the almanac maker Nathanael Low, took full advantage. He went from pious in 1770 to putting a picture of Oliver Cromwell on his front page in 1774.[45] In 1777 the title page of the almanac aimed at the general public said that it was the first year of American independence and proclaimed "let Tyrants rage, and sycophants exclaim, Let Tories grumble, parasites defame . . . Britain's tyrant shall no longer reign."[46] Almanacs could send powerful messages, to be read every day, or as needed, to instill courage.

In general freemasonry in Catholic countries had a harder road to hold than in the Protestant states of Britain, the Dutch Republic, Prussia, and Sweden. Diaries aimed at the French masonic market addressed the order's problems, and in particular the attempts by the Grand Orient in Paris to reform itself and to consolidate its precarious position within the French state. The diary of 1777 gave the new statutes of the order and asserted that they were intended to "eliminate abuses and reestablish the harmony of all the lodges of the Nation." The claim was made that these new regulations would result in the uniformity of our government. But the description belies the reality that the divisions in French freemasonry were deeply social, and that many brothers regarded the new rules as an attempt by aristocratic brothers to assert their control.

Perhaps to inspire unity, the French diary, done by an originally masonic publishing house, then recounted the persecution of the freemasons in Naples. The effort to eliminate the order in that Catholic city had become a cause to freemasons all over Europe. It was widely commented upon in orations and condemned. The almanac for the very next year, 1778, noted that the imprisoned freemasons of Naples had been released. The diary invoked "the Public, friend of reason and humanity," and did so in terms directly borrowed from enlightened rhetoric.[47]

In contrast to the persecution associated with established religious authorities, the masonic diaries invariably embraced language directly associated with the Enlightenment. In 1763 freemasons were told that the summit of their mountain "has been enlightened by the rays of the Light." So infused a brother is "an affable spouse, the pleasure of his friends, the glory of his infants . . . he carries the virtue of the lodge into the bosom of his family."[48] Diaries for the 1780s told their readers that "we have given ourselves the title of children of the light and we nourish wisdom . . . the infant of light regenerates the darkness; he leaves the tomb of vice, by practicing the virtues."[49] Liberty also stood high on the list of masonic virtues, "this precious liberty, which rendered the Constitution of the order so admirable."[50] Also important in masonic rhetoric intended for daily use stood the public good; it rests "in a special rank in the Masonic Republic."[51] Enlightened maxims had now made their way into the vest pocket.

Part of being infused with the rays of the century's new light required the practice of civility. Seldom did any masonic diary miss the opportunity to preach the necessity for "the exterior conduct that the degree of interior civility represents . . . the most essential part of civility is a general goodwill . . . a personal esteem for each other . . . never incivility nor indifference." Freemasons aim to be good citizens, faithful to the laws of the state, and attached inviolably to the prince or the magistrates of the state. The "profession of all the social virtues" stood at the highest place of pride in the masonic sense of self.[52] The masonic interest in architecture became part of an abiding interest in "public utility."[53] The sentiments about civility and order were, however, always laced with caution. Even on the matter of slavery, where by the 1770s we might have expected the freemasons to speak for abolition, the caution continued. The masonic diary urged sweetness in the treatment of slaves; nothing was said about giving them their freedom.[54] The almanacs sought to elevate, to exhort but never to offend the interests of their purchasers whether at home or abroad in the colonies.

There were many journals and books that helped to spread moderately enlightened ideas of reason, tolerance, and public-mindedness. Now we should add to them items as small and simple as a pocket diary. Perhaps it was not accidental that masonic diaries for various years gave the list of kings in the order, or its protectors, and signaled out Prussia and Sweden. Always the masonic commitment to enlightenment and public-spiritedness pledged loyalty to the powers that ruled, especially when they were good to the freemasons. These almanacs reflected masonic society, I would suggest, as much as they sought to mold it into harmonious ways. In France, after a major reorganization during the early 1770s that gave birth to the Grand Orient, the almanacs preached dedication to the center: "masonic people will assemble as a single family, in which each individual will correspond with the common center, and from which the rays from the center will direct each individual."[55] They appealed to men and women who wanted to identify with the state, who were eager to be liked, respected, and promoted into places of responsibility. They coveted the world because they expected it to be good for them, to be a place where desires and interests were met and fulfilled. It was easier to be secular when time could be imagined as being on one's side, a lived state that rewarded its participants in the here and now.

With an almost naive belief in the virtues of the secular, freemasons could invent private institutions within the lodges intended to help mold brothers and sisters, to govern them firmly, but benignly. The penchant for governing, as we are about to see, came easily to men, and to some women, who saw the world and its time as comfortable, accommodating. The masonic almanacs said that "work is a justice; there is no one in all of society less agitated or interested, each of us must thus contribute, all of his forces, to maintain the harmony of all of society."[56] Civic pieties sounded good in spoken and printed orations and diaries. But would the authorities of church and state be as comfortable with masonic earnestness, especially if they saw no need for interventions to insure the public good?

The state, and in many places the church, had law and order as their responsibility; these powers were never meant to be shared with private and secret societies, barely accountable to the sovereign power, often illusive and hard to police. In the troubled years of the late 1780s the authorities everywhere in Europe could also have read diaries with an unmistakable political edge: "one wants to imitate; and the kings, the sovereigns and magistrates have been established; but alas, power will be without boundary, authority without limitations, a slavery absolute; and the mason generally only finds in the lodges the happy alliance of sovereignty and liberty."[57] At that moment in The Hague, Prussian soldiers policed the streets, having just put down a rebellion against the stadtholder.

The occupiers might have been worried about what was being said in the lodges, or at the least, read by the brothers as they went about their daily business, less happy, as their diaries suggest, than they had been in previous years. Their almanacs told them in 1787 that they "are the children of the light, & we walk in the light . . . we have renounced evil, we do good. Thus the good is synonymous with the light . . . [the mason] leaves the slavery of sin, and the tyranny of the passions in order to enter the state of a free man who does the good."[58] It was a statement that could be read with a certain ambiguity. Yet it could not have escaped the Prussian mind that free men could be bothersome to the state, especially one that survived by the force of the bayonet.

CHAPTER 3

Schools of Government

We begin this chapter with a paradox that has never been fully explained. Why in the eighteenth century did an entirely private society, a form of voluntary association—which is what the masonic lodges were—adopt all the customs, habits, and forms of government? One standard explanation has been that because the lodges arose in England and Scotland they simply imitated constitutional government. But that circular reasoning only begs the question, offering no explanation as to why this imitation happened in the first place, nor suggesting any reason for the subsequent imitation or interest that freemasonry sparked on the Continent.

The eighteenth-century lodges have left the most remarkable records we possess for tracing the prehistory of nationally identified formal institutions of representative government, most of which emerged throughout continental Europe only late in the eighteenth or early nineteenth century. That may seem like a startling conclusion, but it is less so when we realize that few places in continental Europe held national elections, and local elections were hardly at the heart of old regime systems of governance. The lodges brought onto the Continent distinctly British forms of governance: constitutions,[1] voting by individual, and sometimes by secret ballot, majority rule, elected officers, "taxes" in the form of dues, public oratory, even courts for settling personal disputes; eventually the lodges even sent representatives to nationally organized Grand Lodges, meeting in Paris, or The Hague, or the capitols of the various German principalities. Unwittingly the

eighteenth-century European lodges functioned as schools for government, local but especially national. Even in the eighteenth century
Dutch Republic, where representative institutions were largely local
and deeply oligarchic, the appearance of centralizing, one-man- one-
vote, representative, national government constituted the distinctively
innovative. Also in the republic in the period before the deep unrest of
the 1780s, the lodges made clear to the Grand Lodge that they love
"our dear fatherland in a time when proud and useless lust for power
. . . egoism . . . intend its downfall." The freemasons display "affection
for the distinguished Government of the Country as well as dutiful
subjection to its administration." But then ominously using the term
Patriotten, given then to the opposition, they said that "real freemasons
are good friends and loyal Patriots." They said that they wanted to help
perpetuate generation after generation of citizens useful to the country,
"hero defenders of Liberty and Religion."[2]

The impulse of lodges everywhere was to identify with government
while in the same breath defining freemasons as "enlightened [those]
who wish to revive our virtues."[3] Note, however, that most lodges, particularly in Catholic Europe, were hostile to clerical orders that sought
to influence government, and hence they were often very anti-Jesuit.[4]
The impulse toward a secular order, to enforce authority as would any
government, can be seen from Philadelphia—where Franklin spoke
about the need for true brethren to be "distinguished by some . . .
special authority"—to Berlin and Moscow.[5] There in the time of Cath-
erine the Great, despite the hostility of the official government, freemasons sought to civilize themselves by the imposition of order and
the cultivation of civic virtues.[6]

The lodges aspired to became virtuous, if secular, schools because
voluntary associations in western and eastern Europe, first in England
and then on the Continent, were populated by literate men impressed
by the process of state formation that they witnessed around them. In
other words, developments at the center riveted attention on the actual
institutions and practices of government. Movement and change at the
core had a magnetic effect; at the periphery it provoked concern, as

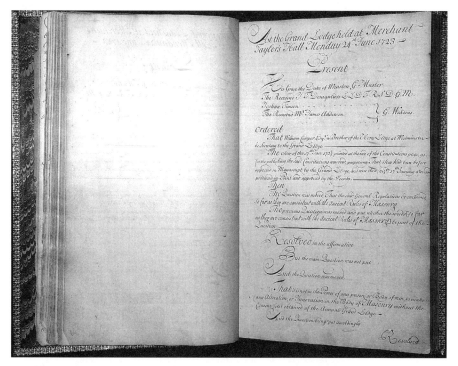

FIGURE 10. The 1723 record from one of the earliest meetings of the London Grand Lodge. London established the first Grand Lodge, which sought effective control over all other lodges. In this meeting it also authorized that its "constitutions" be published. Freemasons always used the term in the plural. With permission of the Grand Lodge of Great Britain.

well as a weighing of the benefits, versus the burdens, that governments could place. Early modern nation building undertaken by kings and ministers led to thinking about nations and systems of government. Not just among great theorists like Grotius, Hobbes and Locke, but among lesser mortals, state officials themselves, merchants, lawyers, teachers, and the ever-present aristocracy. Among the earliest freemasons in both Britain and France we find—not surprisingly—state officials and military officers.[7]

In England the process of state formation, well underway in the sixteenth century, resulted in revolution during the 1640s and 1650s. At issue was the very structure of central government and whether sovereignty would reside in king or parliament. Precisely at that moment the term "constitution" begins to be applied to the governance of groups large and small. Private voluntary associations began to write constitutions for themselves, petition parliament, participate in the turmoil first of civil war, then of restoration, finally to flourish after 1689 in the relatively open society permitted by the revolution settlement. As we are about to see, even a very early history of the masons (written in 1659) made reference to their "constitutions." The settlement of 1688–89 left kings to govern the nation through parliament. It is not accidental that beginning in the 1690s we see an rapid development of all sorts of voluntary associations first in London, then in the provinces: the first four London lodges (and not intended for stonemasons) date from the reign of Anne, if not earlier, as do various reading societies, political clubs, eventually provincial scientific and philosophical societies. The earliest English and Scottish freemasons about whom anything concrete is known—Elias Ashmole, Sir Robert Moray, Robert Clayton, Sir Christopher Wren—were men of letters or science, army officers, politicians, and architects—all with a stake in state formation, all in some sense its beneficiaries. By 1720 there may have been a few stonemasons left in the lodges of Dundee but they are absent—or silent—in English lodges that can be identified in the period. The mercantile, the educated, even the titled, had found a new home, one that they could shape according to their interests.

The process of state formation experienced by these first English and Scottish freemasons during the second half of the seventeenth century was also underway in other parts of western Europe. There too early modern history reveals the growth of state bureaucracies as well as the increase in trade and hence in taxation. Only the Dutch Republic presents something of an exception to this pattern of centralization. In the special Dutch case, aft1aper 1702 and the death of William of Orange (then also king of England and Scotland), there was a growing awareness that the institutions of the central state were weak, in need of reform and renewal so as to better equip them to meet competition from other more powerful, larger, more centrally governed neighbors. Thus whether in Paris or Rotterdam, European men with similar interests and relationships to the state found masonic practices congenial. Not least they came from Britain, widely regarded after 1689 in western Europe as politically advanced, a country with a relatively free press, religious toleration, parliamentary elections.

The argument being made here about the governmental nature of the lodges calls forth an interrogation of masonic records as they illustrate the governing structure, constitutional and representative character of the lodges. Searching Belgian and Austrian, Dutch and French lodges from the 1730s to the 1780s reveals a governmental system thriving decades after the first London lodges came into existence. From those eighteenth-century moments it is possible to go back to the records of seventeenth-century English and Scottish freemasonry, to show the earliest stirring of the constitutional and governmental forms later so vibrant in western European freemasonry. But before we go backward we must first go forward, to the 1780s when crises in various western European states revealed the flaws in the monarchical and centralized regimes put in place over several centuries.

Our first example of the governmental impulse and its fissures comes from Austria and the Austrian Netherlands, i.e. Belgium. One of the best known events in the late eighteenth-century history of freemasonry in the Low Countries was the decision made by the Austrian government in 1786–87 to close various lodges in its western colony. After that date only three lodges were to be permitted in Brussels, and the number of lodges in the Belgian provinces was severely curtailed. This act of repression was initiated in Vienna and coincided with Joseph II's growing realization that just as in Austria, his colony to the west needed to be purged of restive elements. There may have been the recognition that social factions once deemed loyal were increasingly disaffected from the central government. At the same moment other clubs and societies were also repressed.[8]

In 1785–86 Joseph II had initiated a similar repression at home and merged various Viennese lodges, in part as a response to the imagined threat posed by an infiltration of German-speaking freemasonry by the radical Illuminati. What is not generally known is that in the case of the Belgian masonic lodges the purged National Grand Lodge in Vienna assisted in the execution of His Majesty's Edicts.[9]

As documents in the Archives Generales in Brussels reveal, the Viennese Grand Lodge authorized which three lodges should be permitted, closed down other lodges, and drew up lists of members for the remaining ones. In a letter of 23 July 1786, the Vienna lodge proudly informed the Austrian government that "the General Government of masonry is now in conformity with your edicts."[10] On this occasion a fraternal organization, commonplace in European civil society, assisted the state in remaking the contours of another society under its jurisdiction.

The Vienna Grand Lodge acted, as it said, to bring masonic government into conformity with royal edicts. However, no amount of assistance from the private societies in the kingdom saved Joseph II's government from rebellion in its western colony. Not surprisingly, the democratic revolutions in western Europe from Amsterdam and Brussels to Paris went on to spawn new clubs and societies that broke with the established pattern of loyalty, so commonplace to voluntary associations found in the eighteenth century and earlier. By the late 1780s the discontent at large crackled through some masonic proceedings and the loyalty of all brothers could not be taken as a given.

The Viennese records of freemasonry raise the issue of just how well the eighteenth-century relationship between civil society and the state worked. They suggest that in this period voluntary associations could imitate governance quite effectively, on the whole encouraging loyalty to the central authority. Yet in so doing, they could also foster independence and self-reliance among the beneficiaries of the state's expanded role. They could set men to thinking about their capabilities. The general government of masonry. The Austrian government. How many governments were there in this story? Could there have been in Vienna both an Austrian government and a masonic government? Was there an Austrian government and a masonic government in Brussels? What if the pupils in the new schools of government were to graduate into societies they believed to be badly governed? The strength of civil society in the West by the late eighteenth century posed problems for state governments perceived to have failed to foster industry, or promote trade, or wage war effectively.

The same question about the nature of the schooling given by the Austrian lodges can be asked of Dutch freemasonry. Note that in 1756 when Dutch freemasons organized their national system of authority and governance, the Grand Lodge of The Netherlands, they adopted, as they said, "the form" of the Estates General of the Republic. In the Dutch example, the symbiotic relationship between the state and secular voluntary societies manifested itself in the imagined national and masonic community that took shape in The Hague in 1756. But beneath that act of pious identification with the state lurked discontent in some masonic quarters. In the Amsterdam lodge of Jean Rousset de Missy, where many brothers had sided with the revolution in 1747–48 in the Republic, factions stirred. So involved had some brothers been that the lodge, La Bien Aimée, had been closed by the authorities.

Listen to the oration given by Jean Schreuder when Rousset's lodge reopened in 1755: "a little more than a year ago we were still wandering, like sheep with a shepherd . . . without food . . . but strong in courage we united ourselves and after receiving proper and legal authority, we mutually greet ourselves as legal members of a legal lodge . . . a lodge that is the oldest in our city."[11] The law to which the orator referred had nothing to do with the laws of the republic, but rather with recognition given by other masonic lodges. The new Grand Lodge operated a system of governance that came to be seen as legal and that rested on the consent of all lodges that gave it allegiance.

Some years later, the Dutch Provincial Grand Master, de Vignoles, reiterated the characterization of the Grand Lodge's structure as being that of the Estates General. Indeed he recommended it as the best form of governance to German lodges that were having difficulty arriving at a comparable system of national cohesion. He admonished them to adopt an Estates General as "the sovereign tribunal of the Nation."[12] When he wrote of the nation, de Vignoles meant the masonic nation. Just like the Dutch Estates General, where each province retained a high degree of sovereignty, in the lodges the form of decentralized governance permitted each Dutch lodge to retain its independence. The evidence from de Vignoles's description and the information we have about masonic rituals of the period used by the Grand Lodge in The Hague, suggest the same symbiotic relationship between the eighteenth-century Dutch lodges and the Dutch government that we found in Vienna. The Dutch lodges also imitated the institutions of central government, including the ability to make laws, fostering loyalty to it and to one another, and by mirroring the institutions of the state, imitating its strengths and weaknesses.

The efforts to govern in the form of a nation, but to do so within the framework of voluntary association, were particularly characteristic of freemasonry. Many other voluntary associations functioned as if they too were part of imagined national communities, serving the interests of the whole in scientific, charitable, or antiquarian matters. But none, to my knowledge, instituted such an elaborate system of government, one that tied local lodges to national Grand Lodges. They in turn appointed ambassadors and negotiated foreign treaties with other Grand Lodges. As the German philosopher Jürgen Habermas has argued the lodges were one vital piece in the new eighteenth century social experience we call civil society.[13] But they gave a distinctively political implication to its formation and functioning.

The lodges were in many respects different from the other clubs and associations. In a more formal and all-consuming way, freemasonry provided a system of constitutions, elections, majority rule, pluralities, annual assemblies, sealed ballots, even taxes and eventually "courts," where disputes between lodges and brothers could be adjudicated. By 1710 English lodges had also elected a Grand Master and by the 1720s the Grand Lodge in London could claim affiliated lodges in other cities and towns. In 1736 thirty-three Scottish lodges sent representatives to an assembly that created the Grand Lodge of Scotland. They also elected a Grand Master, but only after the candidate had renounced any hereditary claims on the office.

The parallel between state and masonic institutions is not raised in order to accuse the eighteenth-century lodges of attempting to replace this or that national government. Let us leave conspiracy theories in the distant past. By explicit contrast, my intention is to examine freemasonry in London, The Hague, Brussels, and Amsterdam for what the lodges can reveal about the stability, as well as the fragility, of the eighteenth-century relationship between civil society and the state. Before they could flourish, voluntary associations, the matrix of civil society in the West, needed the sovereign state to be firmly in place. If for nothing else, it was the fascinating source of most news and much gossip. In addition, through informal associations, the power of governmental officials could be made more accessible, even if or when their monopolies on power made actual participation in the functioning of the state largely impossible. Yet at moments the associations also provided a refuge, an escape from censorship or, in the case of the lodges, a place for assistance and charity which the state or the churches could not, or would not, provide.

With the state as the structural backdrop, but not as the initiator of assemblies and associations, the lodges could still spend their meeting time discussing just about everything—except politics. The magnetic pull of the political, in the form of the state, encased the social, bracketing its societies and associations off from the religious and the familial. But within that framework, politics did not determine the content of public discussions or the stated, and often pursued, purpose of the vast majority of associations, lodges, clubs, and salons. Whether collecting antiquities, improving agricultural techniques, reciting poetry, doing theoretical science, or paying tribute to the Grand Architect of the Universe, the societies and lodges did their specialized work believing that they were part of an imagined and larger public realm.

FIGURE II. A TYPICAL LODGE DINNER, HERE DEPICTED IN *De Almanach der Vrye Metzelaaren . . . 1781* (Amsteldam [sic]). The description clearly implies that the format should be imitated, and an exact list is supplied on what should be placed on the table and who should sit where.

In many places actual politics remained largely remote from the social, as remote as the courts or the oligarches with whom one might occasionally socialize. Of course, there were plenty of government officials to be found in the urban academies and lodges all over western Europe. But the tacit separation of the social from the political was accepted and even coveted by the voluntary societies. The separation had many uses. It could, for instance, help to consolidate a magnate's or grandee's power and influence. How better to seem approachable than to be called a brother, or to break bread with lesser men, if only for a few hours a month? The separation also meant that, by and large, the state left the societies to themselves.

In the 1740s French and Portugese police arrested and interrogated freemasons, and in Portugal freemasons were tortured for their "confessions." But even in these cases they were released. By the middle of the century in most European countries such persecution had largely ceased. Only in Naples and Avignon, where the Inquisition was strong, did the freemasons run into trouble as late as the 1770s.[14] By that decade such incidents against the freemasons were the exception and rare. Other societies, scientific for example, almost never aroused official opposition, even on the part of the Inquisition.

Once seen as benign by the authorities, societies and lodges could also be a refuge, a place where no one man or event seemed that important. Masonic records in particular often speak of the lodge as a site of tranquility, as a refuge from a hostile world. Social life outside of home, church, town council, guild or confraternity, helped to refocus thought away from financial and personal obligations, as well as away from both commercial and political life. Yet such pressures helped to clear a space for the social in early modern Europe. Trade and commerce were magnets that drew men and some women away from the traditional institutions, from home and church. In the end, however, it was the institutions of governing, and not the practices of the trading companies, that captured the imagination of the lodges just as they fascinated the larger public, the spectators of wealth and power. We can see the search for order and government from the earliest records where the London Grand Lodge displays its concern for officers properly appointed and its own authority singularly upheld.

The impulse to turn toward the center, away from local events or customs, is illustrated quite clearly in the rituals of the Dutch lodges. Like the towns and provinces, the lodges both actually and symbolically coveted their separateness while constantly trying to invent a center, an imagined national community. In 1757 the Grand Master in The Hague, the Baron de Boetzelaer, spoke about "the brother deputies of the respective lodges who have assisted at the national assembly held at The Hague."[15] At these national assemblies the ceremonies placed brothers standing in rows, the first row symbolizing the "Staten van Holland," the legislative body of the province of Holland. Behind them stood the next row of brothers described in the minutes as representing the National Grand Master. Finally, standing in the row in back of them, were the officers of the lodge, visitors, and all the other brothers. So arranged, they joined in communal singing and affirmed their symbolic unity. But were they unifying the nation as well as the lodges? I am suggesting here that, perhaps unconsciously, they were attempting to do both.

The gestures imitative of national government occurred in absolutist as well as republican settings, and the desire to constitute the nation can also be seen in the records of French freemasonry. In 1738 in Paris the Chevalier Ramsay gave what became a famous oration asking that freemasons attempt to create "an entire spiritual nation."[16] In the 1760's, as mentioned in chapter 1, a piece of French masonic jewelry, confiscated from its engraver by the authorities in Brussels, displayed "the arms of France illuminating the attributes of freemasonry."[17] By the 1770s the French lodges were focused on the institutions of central authority. In their proceedings they seldom mention forms of local power or governance, *parlements* or *intendants*. Neither the representatives of the monarch nor the institutions of local power appear to have aroused much interest or identification in the French lodges. When they sought to organize nationally, they were left to invent new forms. They chose to establish a national assembly with each representative having one vote. In the 1770s the French Grand Lodge sought to have a public presence in Paris, partly to allay suspicions.

Yet even in the French lodges for women a new consciousness about governance and political power is evident by the 1780s. Women's orations urged their sisters to be courageous, to cast off the bondage imposed by men and to regard those men who refuse to obey their orders as tyrants.[18] In that same decade a Parisian lodge of adoption filled with ladies of the court donated cannon to the king's arsenal and addressed all the other lodges of adoption calling upon the women to be good citizens and patriots. When we witness the agitation of the early 1790s for French women's political rights, we may justly conclude that women's freemasonry helped to lay the foundation for a new political consciousness, a nascent feminism with democratic associations.

But the French women's lodges were unique in their power and number. In most countries freemasonry remained a masculine prerogative. In the second half of the century, the Swedish king and court were deeply masonic, and the palace served as a setting for many feasts organized by the Swedish Grand Lodge. The fit between membership in the leading Stockholm lodges and proximity to king and court could not have been tighter. Only Berlin to the south rivaled the linkage between freemasonry and the central government. The masonic ambience of Frederick the Great's court in Berlin has often been noted, and Prussian masonic orators were almost sycophantic in their devotion to the conqueror of Silesia. When we see the German Illuminati imitate masonic forms in the 1770s, we should hardly be surprised given the highly political nature of the devotion that Frederick instilled in the lodges.

For our last look at this masonic fascination with the state, whether Dutch or French, we must now finally return to where it all began, to seventeenth-century England. The document discussed briefly in chapter 1, and now found in the archives of the Royal Society in London, sheds important light on the early history of English freemasonry. Entitled "A Narrative of the Free Masons Word and Signs," the manuscript is signed and dated 1659. Its author was Thomas Martin about whom little is known. This manuscript belongs with a family of related manuscripts, all dating from the period of the English Revolution, and these are among the oldest and longest narrative histories we now possess about English, as distinct from Scottish, freemasonry. The narrative provides a largely mythical history of "this Craft . . . founded by worthy Kings and Princes and many other worshipful men." It describes the practices and oaths of working, operative masons, their signs and words, their dedication to the seven liberal arts, particularly geometry. Just as David Stevenson found in the Scottish lodges of the seventeenth century, the document makes mention of Hermes, "the father of Wisemen and he found out the two pillars of Stone whereon the Sciences were written and taught them forth, and at the making of the

Tower of Babylon there was the craft of masonry found, and made of." The document's debt to earlier sixteenth-century texts, now lost, is also suggested by its reference to astronomy. That science "teaches to know the Course of Sun and Moon and other ornaments of the Heavens." For the sun to course in the heavens like the moon requires a pre-Copernican, geocentric universe.

"A Narrative of Free Masons Word and Signs" gives away its contemporary milieu, the 1650s and government by parliament, when it states: "You shall . . . truly observe the Charges in the Constitution." In that decade after the execution of Charles I in 1649, parliament created or adopted laws for the newly constituted republic. Precisely at that moment, voluntary societies with constitutions, however loosely conceived, came into existence. As we saw in chapter 1 the 1659 document mentions a French king being "elected," and it imagines a king from Biblical time who created a great parliament. Given the guild origins of the document it sees the king as providing for unemployable and overabundant male children born to lords of the realm.[19]

Strip away the myths, and what the document reveals is the existence of lodges of working masons who have been charged by a constitution. They have done so in a political universe where both kings and parliaments may be imagined as ruling. Within this context, operative English stonemasons of the mid-seventeenth century identified with the nation-state. They saw themselves as practitioners of the Royal Art, and they also knew that "King David loved the Masons well, and cherished them well, and gave them good payment . . . and Solomon his Son performed out the Temple his father had began, and he sent afterwards Masons of diverse Lands and fathered them together, so that four thousand workers of stone and they named masons and he has 3000 of them which were ordained masters and governors of the work"[20] These English working masons of the 1650s have given their allegiance to a constitution within the context of believing that their livelihood and dignity derives from the state as embodied in royal authority. When educated gentlemen joined the lodges later in the century, they only reenforced the identification with governmental authority. Men who could vote in national elections for parliament more easily imagined government as an entity intended to serve their interests. For them the habits of elections, majority rule, and constitutional government seemed all the more natural and desirable. All those habits were brought to the lodges and in turn transmitted to the Continent. Perhaps now we can better understand why as late as the 1770s French freemasons believed (erroneously) that Cromwell had been the founder of their order.

The point of examining in detail this document of the 1650s is not to try to tease out the political allegiances of English stonemasons during the interregnum of the 1650s. Rather it is to suggest that in seventeenth-century England the relationship between a newly emergent civil society and the creation of new forms of central government were intimately linked. After 1689, voluntary societies, reading clubs, dissenting academies, and a literature full of news and gossip occupied the broad space permitted by the relative freedom of the English press and by the ebb and flow of parliamentary politics. There was a center in London to which society looked. The English social gaze was nascently modern, and it prefigures the role we assign to central government in our own political life, in the content of our newspapers or nightly television, and in the all-consuming nature of modern parliamentary or presidential elections. The English Revolution was the framework within which masonic constitutionalism developed.

Take the constitutional impulse onto the Continent, and I would suggest that the culture of elections, constitutions, voting, and ballots organized its new participants to look at larger and more complex forms of political organization. In the Dutch Republic the typical forms of governmental life were intensely local: *schutterij*, *vroedschappen*, and *landdagen*. Yet none of those local bodies of officials are mentioned in any of the records of Dutch freemasonry with which I am familiar. Where we know much about the political interests of a lodge or its leadership at mid-century, there we find an intense interest in state building and reform. The key figure for our purposes is Jean Rousset de Missy (1686–1762), and his career is worth dwelling upon at some length. He became a minor *philosophe* of the European Enlightenment and one of the leaders of Dutch freemasonry. He was also a revolutionary, and a key player in the Dutch Revolution of 1747–48.

Born a Protestant in France, Rousset de Missy and his family knew persecution firsthand and were victims of the campaign initiated against Protestants by Louis XIV and the Church. The revocation of the Edict of Nantes in 1685 sent French Protestants into the prisons, exile, or forced conversion. The so-called Huguenots of the Dispersion who made their way to the Dutch Republic included the famous skeptic and encyclopedist Pierre Bayle, and on the periphery of his circle, the younger Rousset and his friends. Most important among them was another refugee who had converted to Protestantism and then left France, Prosper Marchand. His vast manuscript collection at the University Library, Leiden, first revealed the extent of Rousset's activities and his role in Dutch political and intellectual life. Unlike many of the refugees, Rousset learned Dutch and appears to have been fluent in speech and translated French works into that language.

Rousset translated and wrote voluminously, and the circle of Marchand and Rousset had contact as early as 1710 with radical English Whigs, in particular John Toland and Anthony Collins. They have been rightly described as the first intellectuals of the Left. Both Toland and Collins were freethinkers and republicans, and as far as can be determined, Rousset translated Collins's *Discourse of Freethinking* (1713) and Toland's *A Letter from an Arabian Physician* (1706) into French. The first advocated freethinking and the second compared Christianity and Islam, finding both to be more or less absurd. From Toland, Rousset got the term "pantheist" and well into his sixties Rousset used it to describe his private beliefs to Marchand. Thus began a lifetime for Rousset in the service, both political and intellectual, of the Anglo-Dutch alliance against France, one that eventually led Rousset to become a prime supporter of the Dutch Revolution of 1747–48, a spy for the Austrians, and eventually a radical reformer who went too far in the eyes of his paymasters. Rousset's immersion in Dutch life and letters occurred within the context of Dutch freemasonry, of which he was a founder and leader until his exile for radical activities in 1749.

No single important philosophical work bears Rousset's name. Indeed his preferred form of publishing was either anonymous or with the use of elaborate initials, such as appeared on the title page of Rousset's French version of John Locke on government: L. C. R. [Rousset] D. [de] M. [Missy] A. D. P., ed., *Du Gouvernement Civil . . . augmentée de quelques Notes* (Amsterdam, 1755). That edition of Locke was almost certainly the one Jean Jacques Rousseau used, and in it he would have found a preface by Rousset de Missy recommending Locke to all who value the fate of republics.

In addition Rousset was a avid journalist; his *Mercure historique* begun in 1724 became a widely read series that critiqued the existing order in the Dutch Republic. It was shut down by the authorities in 1749. All these activities on behalf of the Anglo-Dutch alliance made Rousset a natural choice for the position of official historian in the service of William IV, the stadtholder of Friesland, whom the British assisted in 1747 in a successful revolutionary coup backed by popular unrest. At that moment Rousset's political error was to assume that William intended true reform and that he would back the complaints against oligarchic corruption led by a radical movement known as the *Doelistenbeweging*. For his leadership in it, Rousset lost political credibility with the stadtholder although, even in exile, he remained loyal to the Republic and to his beloved freemasonry. Perhaps Rousset's most original political essay was his account of the revolution, written while he still enjoyed the favor of William IV and the Bentincks, *Relation historique de la Grande Révolution arrivée dans la République* (Amsterdam, 1747).

By common consent historians of what we now call, the Radical Enlightenment, regard one text as its most outrageous, the anonymously published, *Traité des trois imposteurs*,[21] which argued that Jesus,

Moses, and Mohammed were the three great impostors and offered a partial translation into French of a pantheistic work by Spinoza. The Marchand manuscripts reveal the role of his circle, and particularly Rousset, in bringing the book into print, in an extremely rare edition of 1719 now to be found at Young Research Library, UCLA. Many libraries list Rousset as the author of the *Traité*, but most recent scholarship sees one Jan Vroese, a minor Dutch official, as the instigator. Certainly, the text and its many manuscript copies can be traced back to the Marchand-Rousset circle of which Vroese was a part.

No single French language text of the century caused more alarm; even Voltaire was horrified by the contents of the *Traité*. Rousset propagandized on behalf of the text's existence and certainly it expressed, as best we can tell, what Rousset believed in his heart. Significantly at every turn the *Traité* made a political argument. Many perfidies can be laid at the feet of the imposters, but the worst of all indictments concerned their corruption of the state, their attempt to undermine the republic of the Jews. Even in works ostensibly devoted to religion, Rousset as a young man exhibited the political commitments of his maturity: to virtue and enlightenment in the service of the state.

Although Rousset preferred to write in his mother tongue he belongs firmly in the intellectual history of the Dutch Enlightenment. He envisioned a reformation of mores, political practices, and thought; in the masonic lodge men could practice refined forms of government that would be closer to the true republican ideal. His lodge in Amsterdam survives to this day and in 1795 it welcomed the French revolutionaries with songs and toasts. We may safely assume that Rousset would have approved of those evenings when the French appeared as liberators, and not as enemies of the republic, or later as the exploiters as they came to be seen in the time of Napoleon.

Among Rousset's loyalties, aside from his lodges, were his Austrian allies. He saw them as the protectors of the Dutch Republic, and the Diplomatic Revolution of 1756 when Austria abandoned that role must have been a cruel blow. We know that Rousset had masonic contacts in Belgium because he wrote to representatives of the government of Vienna in Brussels and signed with his masonic symbol. Almost certainly those early lodges were allied with the secular authorities against the power of the local clergy. But the Belgian records are preciously few for the period before the 1780s. What little we have suggests that the lodges offered a devotion to the central government in Brussels, and after 1780 an identification (despite his suspicions) with Joseph II and government-sponsored enlightened reform. The Austrian Netherlands possessed webs of local authority, urban and clerical. Urban magistrates may have joined the lodges in large numbers, but the lodges looked to the center, toward Brussels, more precisely toward Vienna. When the Marquis de Gages wrote from Mons to the Grand Lodge in The Hague in December 1769, he identified himself as a true chamberlain of "the Roman Imperial and Royal Majesties." He sent the colors and Great Seal of the Grand Lodge of the Austrian Netherlands, and asked to open formal communication between the two Grand Lodges. He could have been writing to a foreign power; and in a sense, he was.[22]

The aping of central government is nowhere clearer than in the behavior of the various Grand Lodges. Being at the center of nations, they made foreign alliances and treaties. In 1771, the minutes of the Grand Lodge in The Hague record that "England promises not to grant constitutions anymore to lodges within this territory." The London Grand Lodge had declared the Dutch Grand Lodge "free and independent," and recommended that the Dutch lodges operating under an originally English constitution, join the Dutch body. The Provincial Grand Master of England (later to move on to serve the Dutch Grand Lodge), de Vignoles, is thanked at those same proceedings for having seen to it that "each Empire [realm] or State will have its own supervision." This settlement became possible because the British Grand Lodge finally recognized that the Dutch lodges were different "due to the laws of the country."[23]

Part of the Anglo-Dutch agreement had an imperial dimension.

Each Grand Lodge would allow lodges in the other territories to appeal only to the home country for a constitution. The Dutch Grand Lodge approved lodges in the slave colony of Surinam, and indeed had its own ambassador, brother van Hoogwerf, who was appointed foreign deputy Grandmaster. He was instructed to visit lodges in the West Indies, in Suriname and Curacao. He reported back that the lodges there were doing well, and that they were part of "our National Household."[24] Like the nation-state, civil society also aided European conquest and domination.

Although committed to respecting each other's empires, national lodges could nevertheless recognize successful rebels. In May 1782 the Amsterdam lodge, "La Bien Aimée," made a proposal to conclude an alliance with the lodges of North America, now declared independent by this Republic."[25] At that moment, the deputy Grand Master in The Hague begged off a formal alliance, for reasons, I suspect, that had something to do with the tensions of the 1780s between Amsterdam and the Orangist government. The formal recognition of rebels may not have been in the interest of the Grand Lodge. Possibly as part of an effort to solidify the nation, just three years earlier the Grand Lodge had concluded with the German masonic nation "a treaty of alliance which . . . could be very useful, both regarding the general interest of the two Nations and of traveling brothers in particular."[26] There are moments in these procedures when it is not clear which nations, the masonic or the Dutch and German, have been designated.

Western global expansion took its toll on explorers, conquerors, and foot soldiers. For international travelers or military men, the national character of the lodges permitted an appeal that could compensate for the failure of states to reward or care for their citizens and servants. In 1778 a Corsican brother who had been in the French regiment on that island, but who later fought with other Corsicans against the French, found himself and his family in dire straits. Living now in Amsterdam, he appealed for charity to The Hague, telling the Grand Lodge how the king of France had denied him a pension. His appeal, made across lines of national loyalty, asked that the order "render a service all the greater to humanity."[27] The lodges, like the scientific academies to which they were often compared, permitted European men to imagine that they were representing all of humanity. Masonic cosmopolitanism contributed to the creation of Western hegemony, with consequences for women and people of color which to this day must constantly be addressed, negotiated, and ultimately changed. Simultaneously, the lodges articulated an entirely secular and beneficent ideal of brotherly love which they also said pertained to all humanity. As a masonic orator in Amsterdam said in 1752, "A man who does not love another man like himself can hardly be recognizable as a man, because he has no common humanity."[28]

Critics of freemasonry would argue that the Dutch are exceptional and that in France, and in Catholic countries in general, the lodges acted in ways that were subversive. In the 1970s the distinguished French historian François Furet claimed that "freemasonry transformed a social phenomenon into politics and opinion into action. In this sense, it embodied the origin of Jacobinism."[29] The right-wing historian of France, Pierre Chanu, claimed in 1987 that *philosophes* such as Voltaire and Babeuf were united in their "having been masons" and as such in having subscribed to "egalitarian, communitarian and libertarian anarchy."[30] Such views have permeated scholarship on freemasonry and have had the effect of marginalizing it as a subject. Such an entirely biased framework distorts the relationship between civil society and the state as it is revealed in the writings, decrees, and archives of both entities.

A more useful and relevant framework of analysis for the French situation, or any other approach to the relationship of early modern civil society and the state, appears in the writings of Lynn Hunt. She notes that "not all freemasons became revolutionaries, and there is no evidence to suggest that the lodges plotted out the course of the Revolution from closed doors."[31] My research entirely supports that conclusion. But she further describes the exceptionally high participation of

French freemasons in the political life of the 1790s, from royalists to Jacobins. After 1789, freemasons, many of them once left out of the political life of their localities, can be found arrayed in every gradation of the ideological and political landscape.[32] Prior to the revolution, the new politicians had rarely been overtly political. Pushed to the side by the existing system of political power, they were inordinately active in freemasonry, the one institution of civil society prior to 1789 that sought to be both constitutional and governmental.

In eighteenth-century France, civil society was simultaneously drawn to the state and indifferent, even occasionally hostile, to its actual workings. The lodges talked about civic virtue and the need for merit and talent as criteria for true leadership. They were also places where deep social tensions were expressed and adjudicated. More than the English, Dutch, or Belgian lodges, the French lodges were places where violent quarrels erupted. The issues were usually social: which brother had status or deserved a higher grade, which lodge had the purest form of masonry, who would be excluded because of social rank or occupation. The quarrels began as early as the 1760s and went on into the early 1790s. But by 1792 the lodges all but ceased to meet. Other clubs and societies, as well as the dramatic pace of revolutionary events, had made them irrelevant.

The Reign of Terror has been analyzed from many perspectives, and I do not pretend to be able to offer any new insight into its inner dynamics. Yet its unique character seems relevant to understanding the interaction of society and government embodied in masonic discourse and ritual. Eighteenth-century western European civil society could and did focus on the state; sometimes private societies like the lodges could even imitate its forms and conventions. From London to Vienna masonic brothers elected officers, orators, ambassadors, even judges. They voted, taxed, admitted, expelled, adjudicated, formed, and reformed their nations. The institutions of civil society held within themselves the untested but real potential of becoming new kinds of government. All that was required would be a collapse of the state.

When that happened, as it did in France after 1792, the Jacobin clubs became alternative institutions of governance and surveillance. Civil society swamped the state, and government became the work of local committees. Not a single lodge has been identified as the core of a Jacobin club. But the clubs and philosophical circles of the 1790s, as well as the rituals used at the feasts of the Supreme Being, did in some cases imitate masonic forms. These imitative gestures should hardly be surprising. Where else but in the eighteenth-century lodges could an entire system of governance be found, complete with voluntary social gatherings, where an ideology of merit, as well as feasts and rituals, reenforced an identity that transcended the local and reached out to the nation, indeed to all of humankind? The lodges prefigure the Jacobin clubs only, but significantly, to the extent that the Enlightenment prefigures the French Revolution.

When the Grand Lodge in Vienna aided in the suppression of the Belgian lodges, we might imagine that in a revolutionary situation it could have become a very useful and effective instrument of government. But it would have remained merely a mirror of absolutist government, with new authority wielded by men with little or no actual experience of governance. They had been schooled in governments invented in magnificent and closed meeting rooms that excluded the profane. In Vienna the music might have been brilliant, but no setting so intensely private could become an appropriate site for the location of state power.

In 1795 the brothers in "La Bien Aimée" welcomed other brothers who had arrived in Amsterdam with the triumphant French army. Together they joyfully sang "La Marseillaise." Had the system of command emanating from Paris collapsed, would Dutch brothers have attempted to govern along with their French allies? The analysis presented here suggests that they too might have been at the forefront of new revolutionary committees. The experience of the lodges prepared them for the political; the practice of actual state power would require new institutional, formal, and informal settings. Although private and nonpolitical, the Dutch lodges, like their French counterparts, had given men and a very few women decades of experience with elections, committees, orations, mirroring the difficult art of national government. Through periods of decline, revolution, and renewal the practices found in the Dutch lodges served the brothers well; they were prepared to participate as representative institutions slowly and fitfully evolved in Dutch political life.

From the 1790s right up until 1940 and the Nazi invasion, history was kind to the Dutch and French lodges. They could practice masonic government freely and in private without ever having to choose between the pleasures of sociability and the demands of an authoritarian state. What they might not have always realized was how those governmental practices fueled myths and hatreds. In the hands of evil and antidemocratic men, the myths and conspiracy theories would be used after 1933 to imperil all forms of European civil society.

CHAPTER 4

Money, Equality, and Fraternity
Freemasons Negotiate the Market

Eighteenth-century philosophical societies invented modern civil society. Historians and philosophers have related the emergence of this web of autonomous associations, independent of the state, to the spread of a market economy in the West. I will not labor the complex issue of causality between growing market relations and the emergence of the public and the civil. Rather this chapter examines masonic lives in relation to what they tell us about the earliest experience of living as an imagined "equal" in a specific historical context, one increasingly dominated by money, and hence by the market. In the lodges men and, by mid-century, some women, reflected on the moral and civic order in a forum made possible by dues, negotiated their social relations within the confines of an egalitarian ideology, and, not least, sought through charity and loans to mitigate the vagaries of chance and fortune. At the heart of their ideology lay the belief that status within the realm of the civil should be contingent not on birth but on merit. Yet the world around them, while living in the market, thought more highly about people born to riches than about those who struggled to acquire them.

While reserving membership in this most private of the new public spaces to men and some women both literate and prosperous enough to afford the substantial entry fees and monthly payments, the lodges sought to redefine the ideological foundations of social identity, to recreate hierarchy through elections and rituals that rewarded merit and rejoiced in the experience of brothers "meeting upon the level." In the European lodges with which I am familiar—from Scotland, the Low Countries, France, Sweden, and Germany—two monetary practices were universally present: members paid substantial dues upon initiation, then again with each new "degree" conferred, and, of course, annually, if not monthly. In some lodges these dues were actually described as "taxes." This money in turn was meant to cover the expenses of the lodge. Just as important was the second objective: to establish a charity fund to assist brothers who had fallen on hard times, to make loans or outright gifts to brothers or their widows (Mozart's widow being one of the most famous to receive such charity), and wherever possible, to distribute money to the deserving poor, orphans often being high on the list of favored recipients. Beginning in the 1770s the Grand Lodge of France in addition gave money to brothers who were ill, or recommended that brothers who were doctors or apothecaries donate free services to other brothers.[1]

In one of the earliest continental masonic documents charity was seen as the inevitable outgrowth of egalitarian sociability: "The spirit of communication, the sweetness of Equality, of support, of mutual aid . . . all these attributes concur to form the Charity found at the essence and foundation of Freemasonry."[2] The lodges were among the very few, perhaps in many places the only, secular and voluntary societies systematically dispensing charity. They did so increasingly when by the 1770s contemporaries had come to recognize the absolute importance of money and self-interest, and to acknowledge that "the capitalist must have . . . the most powerful motive [for engaging in commerce]; that during his prosperity, the motive is a very strong self-interest."[3] This comment occurred with an atmosphere of economic crisis such as gripped the Marseille region in 1774.

Times continued to be difficult. Men and women freemasons, as well as widows of brothers, wrote to the Paris Grand Lodge and appealed for its "generosity" to relieve them in their miserable state. By the 1780s the Grand Lodge had a committee that did nothing else but dispense charity, sometimes on a regular weekly basis.[4] Most needy brothers and sisters received slightly more than a livre per month "for bread." This was a fairly minimal sum, although sometimes more was awarded. Repeatedly male supplicants refer to the fraternity as a family of which they are legitimate sons. Invariably, they explain, they or their natural families have been stricken with misfortune, disease, accidents at sea, sudden paralysis, limbs lost at war, in short, disasters unforeseen for which they are in no way responsible. "The situation of this brave man is such . . . that he does not merit the bad fortune that he had endured so long in silence. " A Parisian, sister Dupont, wrote that in her extreme need she "dares to flatter herself that her brothers and sisters would bring to her the consolation of humanity." We sense in the letters that the supplicant has literally nowhere else to turn. A widow wrote, "I have two small children. We are without bread, without money." Sometimes the writer is a brother servant who is begging the lodge for work.[5]

Most letters invariably make clear that when good fortune had reigned the writer had been a faithful brother, had risen through many degrees, and always had been a man of merit. Once meritorious and hence, through virtuous conduct, successful, somewhat ironically, only fate and bad luck can be invoked to explain a brother's demise. Many of the correspondents tell that they are far from their place of birth either in France or abroad. These are travelers whose profession, trade, or war-making have taken them from their places of birth—Ireland, Copenhagen, Portugal—and now they are without support. The arguments they give as to why they should be helped vacillate between a plea for generosity, beneficence, in short; voluntary charity; and occasionally the reminder of "the solemn engagement that our contract obliges us to our brothers." After 1789 and the revolution in France, it should be noted, the tone of the letters changes slightly and we find brothers in need more willing to begin their plea with a reminder of "the indispensable duty" of all brothers to help members in need. Still these more self-assured supplicants note their "chagrin" at being in this situation given "the talents, the work" that had gone into their industry.[6] Another brother noted with self-confidence, "my patriotism and my rapport with General La Fayette [also a member of the society]."[7] Brothers were also quick to point out that they had lived by "a probity and a civil and masonic conduct equally irreproachable." In May 1789 one indigent brother asked the Grand Lodge "to procure for the State a useful citizen" and thus to assist him in publishing "mon histoire philosophique."[8] In whatever year, the supplicants were universally humble and woeful, but a few were not shy in reminding their brothers of the contractual obligations that come with virtue and fraternity.

These indigent brothers and sisters of the 1780s and early 1790s tell us that they were caught between two worlds: one, essentially paternalistic, where personal loyalty and charity of rich to poor supposedly prevented the unfortunate from starving; the other, where men and women of merit, citizens of a commercial and international order, believe they are entitled by their social contract (in this instance within their private enclaves) to a modicum of care when in desperate need. From the letters it would seem that no other agency of church or state was able to provide a sufficient net for men and women who, for whatever reason, were in danger, as their letters tell us, of starving to death.

The French lodges were not the only ones to centralize the dispensation of charity. In Belgium the lodges sought in 1779 to establish a general and national treasury for the purpose of dispensing charity.[9] So too did the Dutch lodges in the same period. Before these efforts lodges dispensed charity on a lodge-by-lodge, case-by-case, basis. Thus any lodge's treasury was essential to its functioning and the subject of constant attention. Good manners and timeliness, as well as proper moral conduct, were enforced through a system of fines. In some lodges coins themselves became the actual method of casting votes.[10] In a Dutch lodge of mid-century brothers replaced the older system of black and white "beans" used for voting "by ballot"—one probably imitative of local guild practices—with a system that used different coins in the negative and affirmative.[11] In one other lodge fines were also imposed for "immoral" behavior, excessive card playing, and sleeping away from home in places of ill repute, as well as for lingering at the lodge after it was formally closed. The beneficiaries of immorality were to be the poor into whose "box" the fines were put.[12] In the Dutch republic brothers asked for charity because of "a series of disasters and fatal incidents." Widows, orphans, and "unlucky sailors who until now, after risking their lives to the benefit and advantage of our city [Amsterdam], have no place to go in their old age," in short, fate's most obvious victims, were the favorite object of Dutch masonic largesse.[13]

In the earliest manifestations of European civil society, both charity and brotherhood had to conform to the ideal of merit; only fate was permitted to intervene, and then only on a case-by-case basis. People might rise through their own merit but they could not fall through their own efforts; if assistance was sought, only chance could be permitted to explain poverty. It was the rare brother—but by the 1780s such did exist—who laid claim to assistance by virtue of the constitution, the contract, that bound him to this society. Even then, he sought to make his case compelling, and no amount of detail was spared in describing the misfortunes of fate. In this chapter evidence about the interplay of the vagaries of the market and the response of the lodges will come primarily from Scottish, English, and continental lodges in the Netherlands, Belgium, and France.

Within the forum of a selected and closed "temple," masonic men, among the first Europeans to be deemed equals, self-consciously negotiated their inequality.[14] They came to terms with anciens régimes, oligarchic or absolutist, and for the most part sought a compromise that retained, and in some cases reinforced, social and economic inequalities within an egalitarian framework that rendered them unstable. At its inception modern civil society embraced an idealism about equality that was invidiously circumscribed by the realities of relative wealth and surplus income. It also sought to mitigate that reality by providing charity, but only to members caught out by fate, never by their own malfeasance or incompetence, and certainly not by their birth.

Money in the form of dues, initiation fees, fines for misconduct, charitable funds and loans, was the instrument by which equality and inequality were negotiated. In every lodge the officer designated as treasurer was a key figure who shared access to the lodge's funds only with other officers.[15] And these treasuries could sometimes be large. Dues structures varied, obviously, throughout Europe. Yet all the fees had one common characteristic: they were beyond the means of the artisan or hand worker, all peasants, most servants, and many minor officials.

Some lodges, in Belgium for instance, comprised only the most elite citizens of their town. In Antwerp two lodges in the 1770s were composed entirely of men classified in the top 8 percent of the city's wealth in one case, or the top 17 percent in the other. Initiation in all three masonic degrees could cost about 53 florins; at the time an actual mason, for example, a Belgian carpenter or builder, could hope to earn about 110 florins a year.[16] In France lodge dues directly reflected the means of the members, and as a result the French lodges were often deeply segregated by those financial circumstances. The many lodges of Strasbourg have left an excellent set of records, and not least these Alsatian lodges were among the most socially segregated in the country. Most Alsatian noblemen paid an annual poll tax of between thirty and fifty livres; by comparison, masonic dues were more noticeable and could average ten livres a month. A domestic servant might hope for an income of about three hundred livres per annum. To illustrate the vast distances between the simplicity of the lowly and the grandeur of the great, the lodge La Candeur, which was entirely aristocratic in the 1760s and 1770s, could spend nearly a hundred livres on an evening's reception of a new apprentice at which probably no more than thirty men might be present.[17] Of course, many French lodges were composed of middling men and in turn operated on a far humbler scale.

British lodges required literacy of their members; but, perhaps most important, as early as the 1730s, relative affluence was necessary to pay the dues: a few pounds at initiation, and then a few shillings each month.[18] In addition, the membership records from the earliest official London lodges are noticeably high in fellows of the Royal Society, government ministers, Whig aristocrats, journalists, and not least Huguenot refugees with journalistic or political connections. At a time when the political nation would be defined as the one out of five males who held sufficient property to vote, as well as those literate enough to follow the pamphlet literature that parliamentary politics encouraged, membership in the lodges tended to be confined to such men.

The new private sociability of the eighteenth century rested upon the currency of the market, the commercial order. At its British origin, and in its many and lavish continental manifestations, masonic discourse affirmed "the world"; it was almost utopian about its possibilities. Simultaneously, the lodges sought to hold the world at bay, to distance brothers from the "profane," to offer the corrective to vice, self-interest, superstition, pride, and corruption. Every man when he knocked at the door of the temple and sought his initiation was addressed as a "profane." Only after initiation, executed ritually and through a monetary commitment, did a profane become a brother. Once bonded, the private fraternity sought to create a public space. Within a constitutional structure first created by the London lodges and then imitated throughout western Europe, elections were held, the majority was allowed to rule, "taxes" were collected. In the Dutch Republic, for example, newly elected masters were presented to their brother-electors after what was described as a "public vote, and by being told that they were being presented publicly."[19]

Some decades ago the German philosopher Jürgen Habermas articulated the role played by sociability in the creation of the new public sphere. He argued that the public space being delineated in the eighteenth century was created by and for the European bourgeoisie. The "bourgeois public sphere" was intended to regulate civil society, and it became possible because of "the background experience of a private sphere that had become interiorized human closeness." Out of a more egalitarian intimacy the public sphere arose "as an expansion . . . and

. . . completion."[20] Not only the bourgeois family but also, Habermas believes, the habits and practice of commerce created the "public sphere." With extraordinary insight he argues for its appearance first in England in the 1690s, in the aftermath of the political and economic transformations effected by the revolution in England. And he sees the rapid spread of freemasonry, more precisely, as anticipating the adoption throughout Europe of the public sphere as an alternative to absolutism.[21] In his account the lodges become the first places where "the bourgeois met . . . with the socially prestigious but politically uninfluential nobles as 'common' human beings."Although we do not have to accept Habermas's terminology about the bourgeoisie, especially because it leaves out the many marginal men who were present in the earliest lodges—refugees, actors, in Paris, "a Negro who serves as a trumpeter in the King's Guard"[22]—nor endorse his gender blindness, we can still acknowledge that his analysis has merit. It does not explain why the values of a more egalitarian intimacy produced a public sphere intended largely for men. Nor does it address the phenomenon of the continental women's lodges. But it does point us to the fact that a politically meaningful public sphere—as well as the first masonic lodge—emerged in England during the 1690s, after the establishment of parliamentary government and constitutional monarchy.

Even before Habermas made his greatest impact after 1989, many historians had searched for ways to articulate the relationship between the new philosophical society of the eighteenth century and the origins of modernity. Invariably they have seized upon the political implications of sociability, and either they have been so blinded by their hostility to modernity as to see conspiracy everywhere, or so terrified by the economic implications of egalitarianism as to see communism where, I will argue, liberalism was present. The vast, and largely useless, historiography that treats the freemasons as the conspirators of the French Revolution began in the 1790s with a revulsion against the democratic implications within the revolution. In his history of Jacobinism (1797), the abbé Barruel seized upon the freemasons and argued from their writings that the masonic temple was intended as a public as well as a private space. He believed that as a result, masonic language about equality, liberty, and fraternity bore relation to the radical and democratic phase of the French Revolution, that is, to Jacobin language and deed. From there, however, he went on to construct an elaborate conspiracy theory that linked Jacobins, *philosophes*, and freemasons.[23] Without the paranoia and condemnation, a similar point about the filiation of language was made by the British historian Michael Roberts, writing in the 1970s.[24] In a highly rigorous and scholarly essay, Roberts noted that the slogan "liberty, fraternity, and equality" bears closer relation to masonic language than it does to any other eighteenth-century antecedent.

But as some modern historians would have it, the similarities between the philosophical society and subversion do not end in words or slogans. In the 1970s, François Furet, whom we will meet again in the last chapter, revived the writings of a Catholic historian and follower of Durkheim, Augustin Cochin (d. 1916), and drew from them a new, and disturbing, interpretation of the philosophical society and, in particular, of freemasonry. In the hands of Cochin the conspiracy of Barruel became rarefied into the "machine" enforcing ideological purity and harmony. Cochin asserted and Furet elaborated upon the interpretation that in the eighteenth- century lodges, "consensus was produced by a discussion among equals that did not concern real situations but was exclusively devoted to the relationship of individuals with a set of stated goals." Lost, as it were, in the closed universe of its own rhetoric, the lodge became, metaphorically, a "political party that claimed to embody both society and the State, which were now identical."[25] In this Cold War analysis the masonic lodges of the eighteenth century do unwittingly what the police and clergy of France, and elsewhere, had begun, as early as the 1740s, to suspect might be done. In Furet's interpretation the masonic lodges became the breeding ground for "militant minorities in whom the new legitimacy" might be vested. In Jacobinism, and hence in the philosophical societies that were its imagined antecedent, Furet spied the origins of totalitarian communism.

We can easily concede the point about the filiation of masonic language, ritual, and symbol, and certain aspects of Jacobin rhetoric. Crane Brinton also made it some years ago.[26] But because European Marxists of the nineteenth century laid claim to the Jacobins, and hence to the radical and democratic impulses within the Enlightenment, does not mean that they, and hence Furet, were right. This chapter should demonstrate that the practices of the philosophical society, of which freemasonry was the most important political example, tell us more about the social and economic origins and nature of modern liberal rhetoric and market practices than they do about the communist or the totalitarian. Eighteenth-century private sociability offered a foil to the market, while at the same time, by its egalitarian ideology and dues structure, it mirrored the rules and values of the market.

The lodges reflected the class tensions exacerbated by the growing importance of the market. French aristocratic lodges quarreled with other lodges, including the Grand Lodge, over the status permitted an actor within that lodge; they wished to negotiate their constitutional standing and legitimacy only with aristocratic members of the "mother lodge."[27] Similarly, the French Grand Lodge required assurance that the large number of merchants in one lodge were of the "best reputation." Ideally lodges were to contain a mixture of social groupings, who paid for their admission and degrees within a scale of donations.[28] These degrees were highly coveted and in the Dutch Republic, if not elsewhere, there was a traffic in them by "certain private" persons who made it their profession "to receive somebody for a vile price and clandestinely."[29] Given its international character, however, European freemasonry calls for generalizations that seek not to unravel its tensions and contradictions, either between lodges or between national styles, but, rather, to explain the working of its prevailing and universalist ideology, its egalitarian posture in a world where the market appeared with ever greater frequency. Looking at how the market shaped the lodges, and how they in turn responded to its pressures, may help explain the appeal of its liberal universalism.

THE MARKET ORIGINS OF MASONIC SOCIABILITY:
THE VIEW FROM SCOTLAND

I want now to observe how one of these first experiments in European liberalism actually worked, to visit a lodge at its Scottish origin, and to relate its evolution and practices to the market circumstances in which it had to operate.[30] What follows is the story of the lodge in Dundee, Scotland, culled from its largely unexplored seventeenth- and eighteenth-century archives. It is logical and proper to begin in Scotland, for there we have the first records that trace the gradual evolution of freemasonry from roughly the 1680s onward, its growth out of the stonemasons' guilds into the gentlemanly lodges of the eighteenth century.

Market forces caused that evolution; in their wake most guilds declined and then disappeared. In Britain only the stonemasons managed to make a transition to an entirely different form of sociability. The reasons for their success to this day are not fully understood, but two elements marked the masonic guilds off from those of other hand workers: the relative richness of their lore and traditions, and the rather high degree of skill required of master masons. In effect they could and did function as architects. Thus the earliest nonmasons admitted in the 1640s to the guild in England were men of intellectual and scientific interest, Robert Moray and Elias Ashmole. Later the men admitted were married into families where the father-in-law was a mason, or these nonmasons in some cases had building ventures which they wanted executed, or they possessed the means to help masters initiate such ventures.

The Dundee records are rare for their completeness, although other Scottish lodges also left similar archives documenting the transformation from guild to fraternity. The very richness of these records has led the historian who has worked most extensively with the seventeenth-century records, David Stevenson, to argue (too one-sidedly, I believe) that the freemasonry bequeathed to the eighteenth-century continental Enlightenment was singularly a Scottish invention.[31] By this he means

that the transformation from a guild of stonemasons to a society dominated by gentlemen, if not completely devoid of hand workers, occurred first in Scotland and then spread gradually to England. For our
purposes here the locus of the evolution hardly matters; rather, it is the
process and its outcome that reward scrutiny.

By the 1690s the Dundee lodge had fallen on hard times. Out of
economic necessity, it began quite straightforwardly to admit noncraftsmen to membership. That process was undoubtedly related to
what happened as the town sank from a once prosperous east coast
shipping port to an increasingly impoverished community, threatened
with civil disturbance. Its decline began with the sacking of Dundee by
a parliamentary army in 1651, and continued throughout the last decades of the seventeenth century as the Atlantic trade and the western
ports grew in importance. This pattern was only reversed slowly, in the
last decades of the eighteenth century, with the growth of the linen
and clothing industries. Thus, in the period where we can observe
firsthand the transformation of a trade guild into a gentlemen's fraternity, all but the richest of Dundee's inhabitants negotiated with poverty
and with "ye decaying state of ye Burgh."[32]

A town with a declining population of approximately six thousand,
Dundee possessed about a dozen guilds of tradesmen, all strictly arranged by rank and status. The cloth dyers were last in social rank,
while the masons, coopers, barbers, wrights, and periwig makers were
considered sufficiently skilled to be organized in a cooperative association separate from the other, more menial trades. The merchants were
also organized in their own guild, which held considerable political
power in the town. By the 1720s the masons contributed to it without
being permitted to join. In 1749 a mason applied for admission to
the merchants' guild, but "he was objected to because as exercising a
handycraft, he cannot be admitted a member of the Guild, except he
give over working as a tradesman, being contrary to several Acts of
Parliament."[33] Ironically, that same tradesman would have socialized
with merchants in his lodge by this date. In the world of any eigh-

teenth-century town or city rank or status was everywhere palpable. As they evolved, the masonic lodges of this period reflected those realities, in one sense mitigating them, in another, through conviviality and the rhetoric of harmony and fraternity, obscuring, and hence reinforcing, them.

In the early 1700s the Dundee guild had come to a financial impasse. One solution was to admit nonmasons into the fraternity. Other lodges in Scotland and England had, of course, also admitted them intermittently throughout the seventeenth century. Indeed, the decision in Dundee was only in keeping with what was by 1700 a fairly commonplace solution to the economic problems then experienced by all craft guilds. In 1713 the Dundee town council, "taking to consideration the great decay of the burgh and houses within the same for want of inhabitants, and for encouraging strangers to come and live among us," decided that anyone marrying into a trade family could enjoy "the privilege of a guild brother."[34] Yet obviously the Dundee masons' guild believed that its "freedoms and privileges" within the town were worth a not insignificant sum, although the ten pounds (Scots) membership fee requested was less than the sixteen pounds paid by a working journeyman to procure his "privileges" and status as a master in the lodge.

The Dundee records are clear that preference for admission of noncraftsmen was to be given to relatives of actually "operative" masons. There was a predictably large number of such sons and sons-in-law admitted to the guild during the eighteenth century. They could be of any occupation. By far the largest number of new members who are not practicing masons, but who tell us their occupations, are described as merchants, and also as a clock and watch maker, a draper, a wright, an officer of the excise (1721), a surgeon, and finally, in the 1730s, a supervisor of the excise, a doctor of medicine, a shipmaster, a clerk of the customs, and, most significantly, landed gentlemen of the county who bear the appellation denoting their gentry origin, "honourable." They received the same "freedom"—now uniformly described as "libertys"—and "privileges."[35] The "liberty" now accorded to gentlemen, merchants, and minor officials recalls the distinction, of medieval origin, between the "liberty" of buying and selling in the burgh, once given to burgesses who were also merchants, and the "freedom," generally accorded to those who were free to work at their hand trade.

These linguistic distinctions now occurred while a significant number of operative masons continued in the Dundee lodge. It struggled throughout the century, as did the other crafts, to protect and control the labor of its working members, often against the practices employed by local merchants, and to ensure that members would only employ craftsmen duly admitted to the guild. Yet there is also some evidence of tension within the lodge between the working men and their "betters."[36] The Dundee lodge was quite different from one that met in London in the 1730s. It had over one hundred members, of which not one was a working mason and the vast majority were mercantile by trade.

The tensions in the lodge were the perennial effect of Dundee's poverty, which meant the absence of sufficient municipal funds to repair public works, as well as a dearth of capital to repair "ruinous properties . . . owing to the poverty of the owners." There was also the problem of vagrancy and begging, in other words, of social control. Such social and economic problems occurred, however, within a distinct political culture. As the Whig ministry in London led by Sir Robert Walpole in the 1720s came to control Scottish political life, all patronage came under its purview and under the skillful manipulation of its man in Scotland, the earl of Ilay. No office, no agency of revenue collection, from salt to the excise, was small enough to escape Whig domination.[37] Concomitant with, and indeed augmenting, this consolidation of power was a policy of "improvements," which established commissions to improve fisheries and manufacturing and to encourage agricultural experimentation and innovation. All these factors favored the gentlemen within the lodge who came resolutely to control it.

By the 1730s the lodge was actively involved in promoting public works projects, contributing generously in 1739 to a fund for building a workhouse for beggars and other poor. In 1730 guildsmen and burgesses had joined in petitioning the magistrates to build a new prison, with a local mason promptly volunteering to take down the old one for a modest fee. Culture was also imported into the town, and in 1734 freemasons paraded to the local theater to see a production brought in specially from Edinburgh.[38] Of all the local guilds the masons were most active in a process of "improvement" that was visible in Dundee by the 1730s, despite its chronic economic problems. Even the appearance of famine in the vicinity in 1741 did not stop the town council two years later from putting up the money to hire a "professor of mathematics and book keeping" for the local public school. The gentlemen freemasons in Dundee were not necessarily Whigs, but they did promote the political culture of improvement associated with the Whig ascendancy.[39] It is also worth noting, if only in passing, that the habit of clubbing was more pronounced among late seventeenth-century Whigs in London than it was among their Tory rivals.

More than civic involvement came with the transformation of the Dundee lodge from what masonic histories like to call operative to speculative freemasonry, that is, philosophical as opposed to practiced masonry. What is striking about the process that accompanies the admission of increasingly elite "brothers" is revealed in the new language gradually replacing the traditional guild terminology. In the seventeenth century, guildsmen spoke more often of their statutes and ordinances, not frequently of their laws, and generally the brethren gave "their consent" to the admission of a new member or to the "selection" of their officers. Occasionally, "the mason trade in Dundee being met together have made and constituted" a master to his "privileges."[40] These consisted of the right to regulate wages, settle disputes among members, and be consulted about taxes by the local magistrates. Guilds had the privilege to exercise authority and control in the lodge and in the community, but not to govern. That was the work of local magistrates. Quite suddenly, and within less than ten years after the admission of merchants and the sellers of commodities, the language of parliamentary procedure, and hence governance, makes its appearance. An officer "was by plurality of votes chosen." By 1718 "the members of the mason craft being convened did unanimously elect and choose" their officers, and in 1734 a quorum was fixed. By the 1730s the "freedom" of the guildsman, traditionally the freedom, upon admission, to practice his craft in the town, has been transformed into the "libertys of the craft." At that same moment (1732) "members [were] unanimously admitted and received into the Society [sic] of master masons." This "fraternity" of guildsmen has become a "society" of gentlemen and merchants, now styled as master masons, who vote and elect, and who possess their liberty just as craftsmen once possessed their freedom.[41]

In 1734 the transformation was ensured. The power to govern was placed in the hands of the gentlemen freemasons. The occasion for this shift of authority over the "government" of the lodge involved both money and labor. Money had been inappropriately lent without proper security. Craftsmen not belonging to the guild had been employed, while the quality of craftsmanship of some operative members was deemed inadequate. At the annual meeting of the year the gentlemen of substance were elected as the officers. The Honorable John, master of Gray, was chosen as master of the lodge, and he was also a local agricultural improver. Suddenly language employed by London freemasons and first displayed in Anderson's 1723 *Constitutions* appeared with full force in Dundee. Terms appear that are not to be found in the records of the Dundee operative masons: "the Society of Free and Accepted Masons," the "Hon. Society of the Antient Lodge," the "Laws and Regulations for the better and orderly Government of the respective Brethren." Brothers are charged with the task of assembling "to consider of such Laws and Regulations as shall seem most proper and requisite for the better Government of the Society . . . with full power to them to make and enact in the locked book of the Society such laws as shall seem best for preserving order and unanimity among the Brethren . . . and punishing delinquents of whatever Rank or Degree." A committee was established to do just that.[42]

For the first time in these seventy and more years of records, reference is made in the same manuscript entry to the "secret mysteries of Masonry." It shall no longer be "lawful by any and or number of the brethren of the lodge of this place to initiate or enter any person or persons of what ever degree or quality . . . to the knowledge of the antient and secret mysteries of masonry without first apprising the worshipfull, the master of the lodge." Without his consent a man may not be admitted. In this context the secrets refer to the traditional skills of craftsmen as well as to signs and words used by properly initiated guild masons to signal to one another their status, and hence their right to work. It is significant that only now does emphasis on the "secrets" of freemasonry appear. Secret signs and tokens of membership had been the everyday manner of communicating among craftsmen. The ability to keep the secrets now became symbolic of devotion to the fraternity, of loyalty and probity. That ability to hide—rather than to practice the mysteries—became the only means of identifying a true brother. This social cement was mystical only insofar as it was language memorized out of its original context—it now became words and signs used in the bonding of men who were different from one another in nearly every aspect of their lives, save their membership in a constitutionally governed private society. Eventually the "secrets" of freemasonry acquired a metaphoric meaning, as brothers rose by degrees toward a veiled, yet constantly unfolding, wisdom and enlightenment. Accompanying this process were ever more elaborate, and expensive ceremonies conferring status and honor within the lodge.

The process of elaboration that we have witnessed at work in Dundee by the mid-1730s occurred elsewhere in the Scottish, as well as English, lodges. Gentlemen were admitted and elected "masters" of the lodge. Suddenly, whole initiation ceremonies were created to install the master in his "chair," with overtones of ceremonies used to initiate men into the aristocratic and kingly orders, such as the Order of the Garter, or, indeed, with intimations of royal coronations and court ceremonial. In the 1730s, following the practice in England, Scottish lodges instituted "degrees" by which practicing, that is, operative, and nonpracticing members might be distinguished one from another. Not least, in 1736, the thirty-three Scottish lodges, Dundee among them, sent representatives to an assembly that created the Grand Lodge of Scotland, which in turn elected a gentleman Grand Master, only, incidentally, after he had renounced any hereditary claims on the office. The national government of Scottish freemasonry could now be said to have been put in place. One of its first acts may have been to give constitutional authorization to a foreign lodge that had appealed to it. The lodge was in Amsterdam and its master was the Huguenot refugee and self-described "pantheist" Jean Rousset de Missy.[43] In the Scottish transformation away from practicing stonemasons officers were not only to be nominated and elected, they were also given the power of oversight in all aspects of craft activity. Nominations were now to be held for "the Election" of officers who shall have the power and authority to appoint a quorum "of the Operative Brethren not exceeding five in number . . . to visit and inspect" the work done by other masons. By 1737 "rolls [were] being called and votes marked" and elections were "carried by a plurality."[44]

In every sense power had decidedly shifted into the hands of the gentlemen freemasons, who would oversee the work of their operative brethren. Yet in this instance, and in contrast with the hostility shown to the protective practices of the working masons described in the 1723 *Constitutions*, the gentlemen freemasons of Dundee did continue to protect the "freedom" of their working brethren by permitting only initiated masons to work in the town. Throughout the rest of the century some efforts were made intermittently to restrict the practice of the craft to members of the lodge. The charitable obligations of the lodge also continued to be important, and it proudly maintained its locked pew in the local church. Yet increasingly its records speak of the "liberty" of the freemason as more and more gentlemen, as well as relatives of practicing masons, are admitted to the society.

From the early eighteenth century the signs of increasing literacy also become more frequent. The marks and rough, uncertain scrawl by which the majority of brethren signed their names in the seventeenth century give way and eventually by the 1750s all but disappear—even among the craftsmen who remain. In the 1650s masons spoke of "the blessings of God" and "the better ordering of our Comonwill," and they made reference to their craft as "the calling." In Dundee these same craftsmen invoked the Trinity, opening their lodge in 1659 with words taken from the so-called Old Charges, rules widely practiced by lodges throughout England: "The might of the father of heaven with the Wisdom of the glorious sone and the grace and goodnes of the holie gost be with us at our beginning."[45]

Concomitant with evidence of increasing literacy, and fewer operatives, the old religious language all but disappears. In its place stands reference solely to the Newtonian Grand Architect of the Universe. In the 1740s prospective candidates for admission as operatives were tested by "an Essay of an Architecture," now, however, requiring an arithmetic knowledge of Ionic proportions. The imposition of order extended from a simplified conception of the deity to sound fiscal management of the lodge and came to include correct social behavior, and even the professionalism of skills. Fines were occasionally extracted for infringements of the rules concerning employment. By the same token, money was also lent at interest to assist in business ventures, with the lodge operating at moments like a bank, an institution that did not come to Dundee until the 1760s.

In this fascinating instance the consolidation of elite culture, a process historians have traced as under way from well back in the seventeenth century, included the assimilation and transformation of one of the most representative institutions of early modern European popular culture. The guild, complete with its myths and rituals, has been embraced only to be transformed. And its most binding and potentially subversive practice, secrecy, has been given new meaning. Knowledge of the secrets delineated brothers by their degrees; it also enveloped their private association and made it special. For others in a different setting, it may also have made it suspect.

A direct evolution out of its seventeenth-century predecessor, the lodge in Dundee might easily be imagined as vastly different from its continental counterparts of the 1730s and beyond. Indeed, in some respects it differed from many London and provincial lodges because of the large number of operative masons remaining in its ranks. Yet after 1734, at their core, the practices and ideals of this private society in Dundee—as revealed in the language it employed—were not fundamentally different from those elaborated upon by the London *Constitutions* (1723) and in turn imitated with greater and lesser degrees of imagination by countless European lodges. The importance of the Dundee lodge is that it permits us to watch the unfolding from guild to fraternity.

The emergence of a new private society modeled on—indeed, deriving from—the masonic guilds of medieval origin should be understood in relation to an important moment in the history of European political and economic development. For much of European urban history guilds of craftsmen, and even of merchants, provided, as one historian aptly describes it, "the counterculture to civil society." The guilds were vital participants in town and city life; they functioned to protect their members from the vagaries of the market and from the power of the great magistrates, lay and ecclesiastical. Their understanding of freedom and equality was more protectionist and collective than it was individual and purely market. Yet with these qualifications the guilds also played a regulatory role in the commercial life of any city, operating both protectively and coercively in ways that have been described as "ideal . . . to police the workforce."[46] The guilds regulated who might practice "his mystery," that is, the skills of a particular craft at any given moment and place. The relationship between the guild and the free merchant was partly adversarial, partly collaborative. Guilds might administer the policies of local magistrates, but they did not make those policies, although they might indeed be carefully consulted.

In early eighteenth-century Britain there was nothing "countercultural" about the new speculative lodges. They embraced the rhetoric of constitutional authority, of the magistrates seated in Parliament. The emergence of these private societies suggests a new political mentality striving for expression within a particular economic, that is, market context. We have arrived at that moment when a political nation exists within one of the European national states. This nation, in possession of voting rights, governed self-confidently in tandem with an old aristocracy and a constitutionally limited monarchy. In the cities the mercantile elite no longer needed guilds for their protection; in the countryside, the landed gentry expressed their political interests through parliamentary elections. In town and city the power of the old guilds to regulate wages and labor had now been broken. But the collectivist definition of liberty and equality inherent in guild culture could be given new meaning. It could now pertain to the aspirations of the political nation. Voters and magistrates could meet within the egalitarian shell provided by the guild shorn of its economic authority and in most cases of its workers. In the new masonic lodges urban gentlemen, as well as small merchants and educated professionals, could practice fraternity, conviviality, and civility while giving expression to a commonly held social vision of their own liberty and equality. They could be free-marketeers while hedging their debts. By bonding together through the fraternal embrace, they sought refuge from harsh economic realities if bad fortune made poverty seem inevitable.

CHAPTER 5

Women in the Lodges

Our attention must now focus on gender and French freemasonry in the century of light. The reason is simple: the eighteenth-century records for French lodges of both women and men are richer than anywhere else in Europe and America, at least as yet discovered. Of course, in the Anglo-American world female participation in lodges, as opposed to affiliates and auxiliaries like the nineteenth-century Eastern Star in America, was strictly prohibited. Gender exclusion now plagues contemporary freemasonry in both the United States and Great Britain, where numbers in the gender-segregated lodges continue to fall. So seriously do some contemporary American freemasons take the prohibition against women as sisters that when the Grand Master of France addressed his American brothers in the early 2000s he had to prove the legitimacy of the Grand Orient by asserting that it had never initiated women. It is sad, that the declaration had to be made, more sad for the historical record, that he obscured the reality of a vibrant freemasonry for French (and other) women from the eighteenth century until today.

Just about everything concerning freemasonry in France has been controversial in the era after World War II (and well before). Designated as contentious—as soon as it migrated from Britain into Catholic Europe in the 1730s—freemasonry was traditionally written about either by devotees of the order or by its critics—generally those on the Right.[1] Had they but known that lodges could also act as places where women expressed their sense of themselves, even their sense of equality, then the hostility would probably have been even more intense.

Enlightened attitudes were sought and experienced by rank-and-file followers, generally from the professions, the military, and lesser aristocrats, who joined the French lodges in large numbers from the 1760s onward. They coveted improvement, intellectual stimulation, toleration, and confirmation for their achievements. Initially, the originally male lodges "adopted" women—to use masonic parlance—and gradually women joined what became known to both women and men as "lodges of adoption." The process of gender integration appears to have been underway as early as the 1740s, and in 1745–46 we have the first concrete evidence from a women's lodge working in Bordeaux. As the Bordeaux records tell us, the entrance of women into the lodges provoked controversy. For example, a clerical member of the Bordeaux lodge, the curé of Rions, "was condemned . . . for his extraordinary indiscretion . . . to have led women into the lodge . . . and for having said that he would voluntarily pay . . . 3 francs for making it possible for them to see the lodge."[2] He faced a three-month suspension. Whatever the priest's motives and his relationships with women, the issue of women in freemasonry would not be easily resolved.

Women surfaced earlier in the life of *bordelaise* freemasonry than seems to have been the case at any other European site, as far as we know. A brother announced that women were holding their own lodge meetings in the town, and he called them "des Soeurs de l'Adoption." This would not do, the lodge decided, and in its wisdom moved to prevent it. We doubt it was successful. Women's freemasonry flourished in eighteenth-century France, and brothers were largely powerless to stop it. But they could refuse to recognize mixed lodges, or lodges of adoption.

But the French were not the only lodges where women found a place. Until this record from Bordeaux came to light, the earliest known European women's lodge had been held in The Hague in 1751.

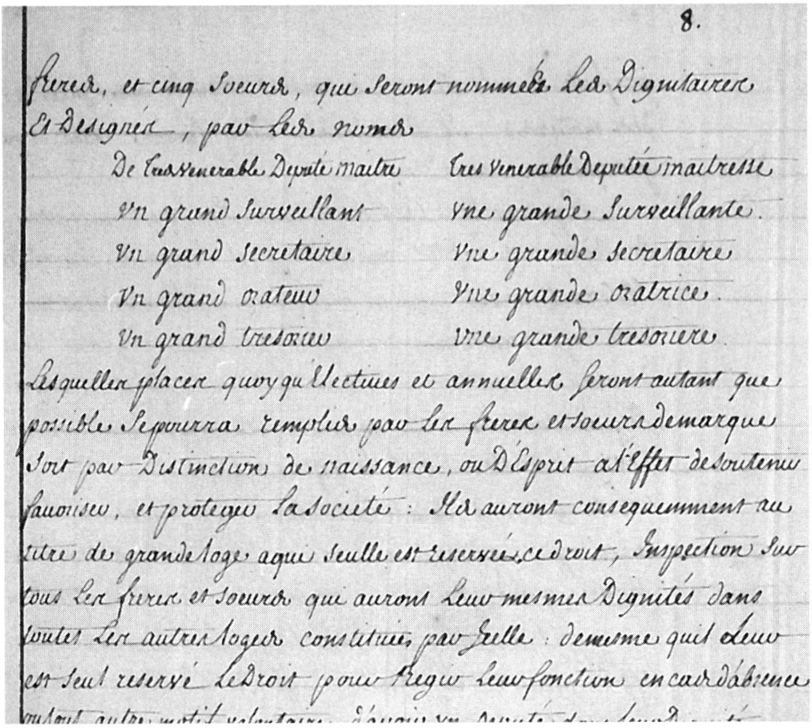

8.

freres, et cinq Soeurs, qui Seront nommés Les Dignitaires
Et Designés, par Leurs noms

De Tres venerable Deputé maitre — Tres Venerable Deputée maitresse
Un grand Surveillant — Une grande Surveillante.
Un grand Secretaire — Une grande Secretaire
Un grand orateur — Une grande oratrice.
Un grand tresorier — Une grande tresoriere.

Lesquelles places quoyqu'Electives et annuelles, seront autant que
possible Se pourra remplies par les freres et soeurs demarque
Soit par Distinction de naissance, ou D'Esprit a l'Effet de soutenir
favoriser, et proteger la societé: Ils auront consequemment au
titre de grande loge aqui Seulle est reservé ce droit, Inspection Sur
tous Les freres et Soeurs qui auront Leur mesmes Dignités dans
toutes Les autres loges constituées par Jelle: demesme quil Leur
est Seul reservé LeDroit pour Regir leur fonction en cas d'absence

FIGURE 12. The manuscript "Livre de Constitutions" makes the point about the search for gender equality in the "Grand Lodge of Adoption." MS 4686 from the archives of the Grand East. With permission of the masonic library, Prins Frederik Cultural Masonic Center, The Hague; copyright Grand East of the Netherlands.

There actors and actresses of the Comédie française had joined with local Dutch gentlemen to create a mixed lodge welcomed by the other, male lodges.[3] Officers could be both men and women, and as the 1751 record was written in French, the gendered nouns made the point: le Maître and la Maîtresse, and so on.

The Dutch Grand Lodge approved of what were known as lodges of adoption, namely the creation of masonic social spaces into which women had to be adopted as they were not naturally born to inhabit them. The Grand Master, the Baron de Wassenaer, signed the book of its constitution as did the other brothers and sisters. If surnames are a

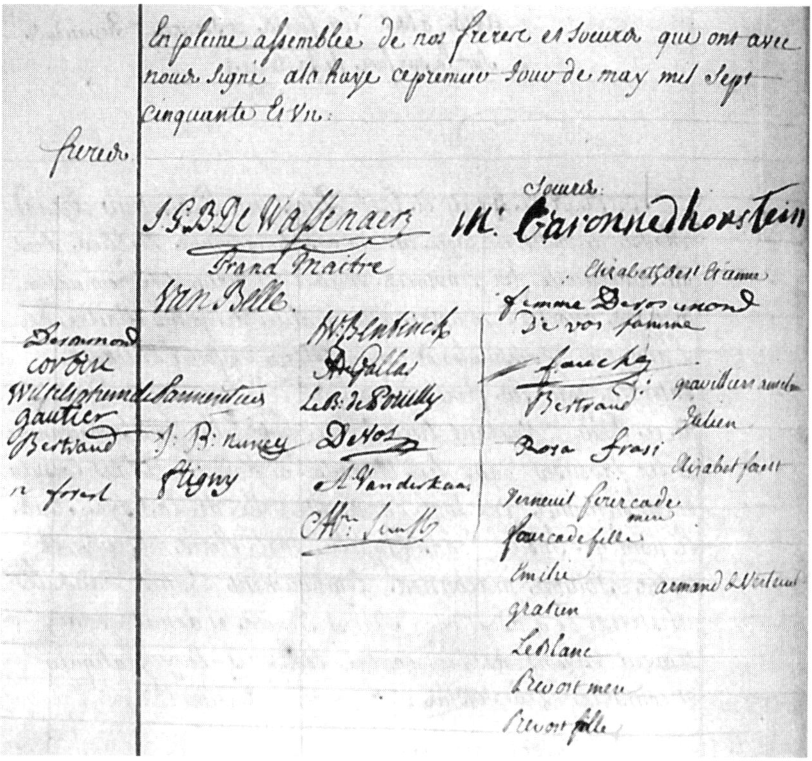

En pleine assemblée de nos freres et soeurs qui ont avec nous signé a la haye ce premier jour de may mil sept cinquante et un:

freres

Soeurs:

Grand Maitre

W. Bentinck

Bertrand

Rosa Frasi

Julien

gautier

Le Blanc

Figure 13. The brothers and sisters in The Hague signed their "book of constitutions" on 1 May 1751. With permission from the masonic library, Prins Frederik Cultural Masonic Center, The Hague; copyright Grand East of the Netherlands.

guide, the sisters were from many parts of Europe, with "Rosa Frasi" suggesting an Italian actress and "De vos femme" possibly belonging to the wife of M. De Vos from France. The signature of William Bentinck in that year is also significant. He had become a trusted adviser to the new stadtholder, William IV, who had been put in place as a result of a revolution in 1747–48. Bentinck represented British interests in the Dutch Republic, and his father in turn had been the trusted confidant of William III, who became king of England, also as the result of a revolution—that one in 1688–89. We can only speculate about the implications that may have been seen in this particular lodge, formed at the moment when the wife of the stadtholder, Anna of Hanover, was at the height of her political influence. Aside from their politics, the men in the lodge were from the highest reaches of Dutch society.

In Bordeaux, by contrast, the issue of women's membership became instantly contentious.[4] Clearly some brothers, perhaps lead by the local priest, thought that mixed lodges were a good idea; a majority disagreed. Thus began a controversy about the public role of women in civil society that continued until well into the last century. Yet we know that in 1775 a lodge of adoption is mentioned in the city, and the following year yet another such lodge was established. In the second, La Loge l'Amitié, the duchess of Chartres and several other noblewomen were admitted. Generally but not exclusively the French lodges for women featured the high-born, even the titled.

Lodges for women signal an important social moment in the history of early modern gender relations. These, like their male counterparts, were not simply social clubs. Voting in elections, dues collection, orations, and officerships were an inherent and formal part of the public life of any lodge. By the 1740s in western Europe women wanted to do such governing-like things, and some men approved, while others vehemently disliked public roles for women and the independence that went with them. Bear in mind that the freedom of women in public remained a fraught issue in the West until well into the nineteenth century. Only then, in Britain, was the need even for public lavatories for women "generally recognized."[5] Late in the eighteenth century women's lodges became all the rage in France, and while both men and women had voting rights, at least one lodge demanded that women could not meet without men being present and that pregnant women not be allowed to attend.[6] But just as important as voting may have been the role that charity played in masonic lives. Writing later in life, sisters talk about belonging to lodges as early as the 1750s. In that decade Sister Dupont was adopted into a lodge and she praised the interest that her brothers and sisters had in the welfare of humanity.

Many years later, and in a poor state of health, she in turn asked for its assistance.[7]

THE GEOGRAPHY OF WOMEN'S FREEMASONRY

A map of French women's freemasonry, including only those lodges for which firm evidence exists, should demonstrate the quantitative strength of female participation in the movement. Women's early membership in the French lodges was distinctive both in numbers and visibility. Elsewhere, women had been effectively excluded from the brotherhood as it swept through Europe and much of the rest of the colonial world by the 1740s. The highly contested but real pressure to include women in lodges in France was the notable exception.[8] Despite the 1723 constitutional proscription against women members, which the British Grand Lodge sought (then as now) to enforce at home and abroad, there was an impressive number of well-established French mixed lodges by the 1760s. Interestingly enough, the terms *maçonnerie des dames* and *maçonnerie des femmes* were used to describe the new integrated masonry. As the map indicates, female lodges grew steadily in number. Their popularity also increased among the upper classes, and lodges began to take on distinct characters of their own. In 1774 the Grand Orient in Paris officially recognized them as masonic organizations. It was the newly reconstituted governing body of French freemasonry. By the 1780s, the women's lodges had become so popular that a new edition of one adoption ritual book was being published annually. During 1787 six editions were published.

From the 1750s to the 1780s women's freemasonry was never a static institution. Rather, as women came together regularly behind the doors of their lodges, they grew in confidence, power, and awareness. As we are about to see, women's freemasonry of the 1780s bore only an outward resemblance to the freemasonry of the earliest decades.

THE RITUAL LIFE OF THE WOMEN'S LODGES

Once the doors of the lodges of adoption swung shut, the members were, in a sense, sealed off from the outside world. With their elaborate

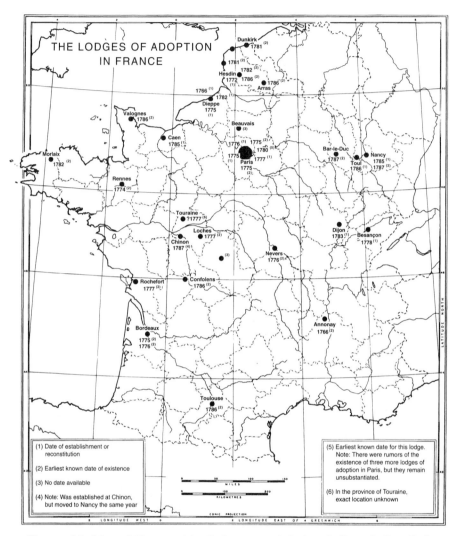

FIGURE 14. Map of France with all the women's lodges indicated. Supplied by the author.

rituals and their secret signs, words, tokens, costumes, aprons, trowels, and jewels, the female masons, like their brothers, could live a make-believe existence; in their constitutionally framed polity, the lodge could become whatever they decided to make it. What they developed in four decades was remarkable, as a cursory look at their rituals will show: the women increasingly established their own identities, and power was transferred from male to female members. When entering the world of eighteenth-century masonic life the historian must assume a willing suspension of disbelief. How else are we to understand why women and men would devote many hours a month, spend lavishly in the process, and covet the opportunity to participate formally in quasi-religious, yet secular ceremonies that we can only dimly imagine as meaningful and satisfying?

The life of any freemason was (and is) governed by the degrees held in the lodge, indicating his or her progress through rituals designed to mark each stage in a passage toward wisdom and knowledge. The degrees had their origin in the Anglo-Scottish guild ceremonies. In earlier times they marked a working mason's initiation into the guild, then his passage from apprentice to journeyman and finally from journeyman to master. By 1710 the three degrees inherited from the original guild structures were being transformed by gentlemen freemasons in Scotland and England into purely symbolic insignia of masonic status, complete with passwords and "secrets." Originally, of course, the "secrets" referred to nothing more than the skilled knowledge possessed by a working master mason. The mason's "word" was simply a device enabling guildsmen far from home to prove their membership to other brothers. But by the middle of the eighteenth century the secrets had expanded to include new words, symbols, and rituals, culminating by midcentury on the Continent in a system of thirty-three degrees in some lodges; others had fewer and different rituals. British lodges officially affiliated with the Grand Lodge of London never entirely accepted these elaborations, but the majority of European lodges honored the original masonic rituals, degrees, and symbols more by imaginative breaches than by rigid fidelity.

The lodges for women were no exception to this pattern of innovation. The earliest extant ritual intended for women's participation anywhere in Europe is that for the Loge de Juste in the Netherlands, dated 1751 and written in French; it survives in The Hague and I have reproduced early in this chapter its signature page. Although it is impossible to know whether, and how closely, its ritual resembled contemporary procedures used in the French lodges, one can assume that it was reasonably representative. Certainly the women in the lodge traveled extensively, and the Comédie française in The Hague (in which they were either players or leaders) often followed the repertoire performed by its more famous namesake in Paris. In addition, French mores and tastes had captured the imagination of Dutch elites, and the nontheatrical Dutch women and men also found in the lodge were to that manner born. Thus the ritual used by the Loge de Juste is particularly useful as a point of comparison with later rituals, allowing a glimpse into the earliest adoptive lodge procedures and displaying certain elements that were not present in later French rituals. The lodge, by the way, was named in honor of the Grand Master of the Netherlands and received a subsidy from the Grand Lodge.[9]

If women were to have control over their own form of masonry, they needed a separate ritual identity. As long as they shared a forest of symbols with men, it would be more difficult to use the ritual as a vehicle for the expression of their ideals. The ritual of the Loge de Juste should be seen in retrospect as an interim one, not exactly like typical men's ceremonies but as something that could be developed into what became the standard women's ceremony. There were more symbols borrowed from men's freemasonry than there were in later women's rituals. Rather than use biblical symbols, the sisters and brothers of the Loge de Juste spoke in builders' terms, using words reminiscent of the ceremonial life of the male lodges. Yet even in this ritual, and in an accompanying songbook complete with an oration on equality, the men and women of the lodge made efforts to grapple through thought and ritual with the meaning of "equality." In the aftermath of women's admission into a private society that sought to define and instill egalitarian mores, a ritual and core of officers that required equal participation among men and women seem only appropriate.

No ritual text contemporaneous with the one in The Hague has yet been found in a French archive. The earliest extant French ritual for women was written in 1763 by the Count de Clermont, Grand Master of French freemasonry. It became a prototype for all subsequent female masonic rituals. Sections of the original manuscript ritual have been crossed out and the wording changed, leading us to believe that updates were made from year to year as members saw fit. It is difficult to compare the four-degree ritual written by Clermont with the three-degree Scottish ritual of the Loge de Juste since different degree levels are involved, but there are certain important similarities and differences that can be isolated.

Clermont's ritual, unlike that of the Loge de Juste, seems to have been designed for women only, and it stipulated that men had to have attained at least the second degree of freemasonry to be considered for membership in a lodge of adoption. Between 1751 and 1763 the form of the degree initiation did not change: the presiding officer questioned the candidate to ascertain her worthiness to join, tests were administered, the candidate took an oath, and two of the officers recited the catechism containing the degree knowledge. But unlike similar male initiation rites, this 1763 ritual went out of its way to make clear that women, despite their penchant for curiosity, have had a favor conferred on them. In the initiation into one of the higher degrees, the story of Lot's wife and her self-destructive curiosity about the city of Sodom was then invoked, serving to caution both men and women about lust and license.[10]

Generally the women's lodges, beginning with de Juste, concerned themselves with virtue and personal character—themes that were also discussed in the male lodges, but never as prominently. The latter focused more on the virtues associated with public service and governance and less on private moral improvement. Nevertheless, the idea of purity in the Garden of Eden was a central theme in both male and female masonry. Part of the order's belief was that through freemasonry a member could somehow regain the pristine beauty and innocence of humans before the Fall. The engraved rituals that appear in chapter 2 display this theme of rebirth. This belief seems to be reflected in one of the first three-degree ceremonies at the 1751 Loge de Juste, and it

FIGURE 15. This engraving of the Garden of Eden, probably from a painting, formed the backdrop to a woman's reception into the second masonic degree. Only in these women's lodges was the story of Adam and Eve retold and Eve's guilt removed. From *L'Adoption ou la maçonnerie des femmes* (The Hague and Geneva, 1775), 27. With permission of the masonic library, Prins Frederik Cultural Masonic Center, The Hague; copyright Grand East of the Netherlands.

was also an important part of Clermont's second degree ceremony. In their basic symbols and practices, then, the Loge de Juste and the French lodges of Clermont were related. A distinct set of themes identifies them both as masonic organizations, searching for virtue and new masonic meanings through rituals that used biblical and building symbols.

The differences between the De Juste and Clermont lodges, however, were as dramatic as the similarities. While both rituals involved decorations and vocabulary derived from the building trade, these holdovers from the men's ritual were less important in Clermont's later ritual. One interesting moment in Clermont's ceremony occurred when the candidate swore her oath with one hand on a compass and the other on the Gospels. This oath-taking apparatus, combined with the heavy infusion of Old Testament symbols and certain references to reason and enlightenment in the ceremony, seems to indicate an uncertainty about the spiritual foundations for female masonry at this date. Was it a builder's ceremony with Enlightenment overtones like the men's lodge ceremonies? Was it biblical in the Old Testament sense, which could be made compatible with the Enlightenment's fascination with the ancients but not easily reconciled with the building symbolism in the men's lodges? Or was it religious in the French Catholic sense? The Old Testament symbols proved most enduring. Particularly significant was Clermont's thorough integration in the degree ceremonies of the symbol of Jacob's ladder—a symbol that had been added to male masonry a few years earlier in the Kadosh degree (a higher degree adopted by the French from the German Strict Observance rite).

If we remember the significance of Catholicism, particularly in the lives of educated elite women who, when not taught at home as they generally were, received instruction outside the home from nuns, we can begin to see the importance of the transformation of the biblical stories taken up and used approvingly by female freemasons. Theologically, the story of Eve's temptation and fall had been used to justify women's inferior status and in particular their inability to officiate as clergy or leaders. As an imaginative resource the story worked to reinforce images of female lust, intemperance, and seductiveness. But in the adoptive lodge rituals, the myth of Eden is confronted and the story reworked. In the early versions of the Eve ritual brothers remain central, even responding or speaking for their sisters. But what they have to say to their sisters in masonry subverts the myth: you are in the Garden of Eden, you eat the fruit "but not the pip that represents the germ and the seeds of vice."[11] In another of the Clermont rituals, the Grand Master cuts an apple in two with a trowel, removes the seeds, and gives the rest of the apple to the candidate to eat. As she eats the apple, he says, "Bear in mind, my sister, that the laws of masonry forbid you to eat too much of any apple's seeds because apple seeds are the origin of the forbidden fruit."[12]

The lodge now represents the Garden secularized, where love of family, friends, citizens, states, and country is taught, where women are adopted who were once banished unjustly out of ignorance. As in the Lot ritual, such lodges repudiate the mysteries and "indecencies" associated with Saturn, Bacchus, and Priapus.[13] By the 1780s, however, the obsessive concern with license and decorum largely disappears. The biblical references remain, but the adoptive lodges now become places where women swear loyalty to king and faith, *roi et foi*. On becoming "masters," the women swear devotion to the Catholic religion and their prince while they also ritually and triumphantly slay the serpent.[14]

While the men's lodges presented themselves more self-consciously as schools of government where brothers learned to vote, give orations, live under constitutions and majority rule, accept women's friendship, and merit "l'estime du public,"[15] women's lodges could use the same universal masonic structure to aspire toward an overt political life for their members. Their aspirations prefigure the women's republican clubs of the early 1790s. The political life being invented in the lodges is not simply about personal, polite power expressed through salon conversation and writing; it is also about the state, about forms of constitutional and legal life. The reason being expressed here is closer to that of the state than it is to an imagined "masculinist reason," a phrase invoked by some feminists in order to denigrate the rationality proclaimed by the Enlightenment.

Masonic rituals had for many decades expressed sentiments about the polity. Clermont's ritual did not originate in his own imagination. The French masonic historian André Doré undertook some detective work on its genesis and believes that it came from a 1744 publication entitled *Le Parfait Maçon ou les véritables secrets de quatres grades d'apprentices, compagnons, maitres ordinaires et écossais de la Franche-Maçonnerie.*[16] This 108-page book was one of the first in a series of "revelations" or "exposures" of the freemasons that circulated during the 1740s, some of which were translations of English texts. *Le Parfait Maçon* contained biblical themes and omitted the sequences from the building of Solomon's Temple that were central to male masonry. It also included one of the earliest continental references to Scottish-rite masonry, and the political message the rite evoked was seldom neutral.

No subject in eighteenth-century European freemasonry is more complex and confusing than the Scottish rite. The Grand Lodge of London never liked innovations, particularly any addition of new degrees to the original three by which official British freemasonry to this day is characterized. But the so-called Scottish rite posed a special threat to its conservatism. Scottish rites had nothing to do with Scotland per se, but rather involved the widespread masonic belief that the lodges there were either purer or more egalitarian than the Grand Lodge with its largely oligarchic leadership. Hence, espousing "Scottish" freemasonry was generally an act of defiance that could take many forms. As it was exported to France (possibly by Jacobite refugees), it could then be used to represent the aristocratic reaction toward the state led by the Grand Lodge after 1773. New degrees could mean status and hierarchy in a purer, more cerebral freemasonry. Similarly, egalitarian reformers, both women and men, could use ceremonial innovations associated with the Scottish rite to express hostility toward the authorities, and by the 1780s that impulse had turned many French lodges into hotbeds of dissent.[17] Indeed, among all the western European countries and periods in which we have studied masonic records, only France in the 1780s presents a portrait of lodges out of control, of incessant and unrelenting social hostility in and between lodges. In archives that have largely been underused by recent social and political historians, one can take any French city—Montpellier, for example—and find dissent and deep hostilities surrounding issues of class and status. These hostile sentiments were being expressed in letters and orations from almost every lodge by the late 1770s and escalating in the 1780s.[18]

New rituals and forms of masonry allowed for the expression of dissensions. Predictably, once the lodges became implicated in the revolution their critics seized on the decades of innovation associated with the Scottish rite. The earliest surviving French attack on the lodges dates from the autumn of 1789, and specifically singles out Scottish-rite freemasonry as being responsible for the revolution. The Scottish lodges had become "red lodges," "clubs de la propagande," where all social and religious mores were contested.[19] I suspect that the royalist and probably clerical author of the attack did not even begin to imagine the gender roles that the lodges could also subvert.

The lodges of adoption were almost invariably identified with Scottish-rite masonry.[20] By the license it gave to innovation, the Scottish rite could be infinitely malleable. But to this day in masonic circles innovation is the subject of controversy. Because of its ties to modern and more orthodox freemasonry, Doré's study of these rituals was deeply suspicious of masonic innovations and began with the assumption that women were taken in by them—that they were given meaningless rituals to mollify them. He is almost surely incorrect in this assessment, which echoes the disdain that twentieth-century freemasons have generally brought to the study of eighteenth-century Scottish-rite innovations. His research and analysis do not transcend the worn-out framework built up by nineteenth-century masonic historians who had no knowledge of, and perhaps no interest in, factors outside the narrow confines of lodge history. Unfortunately—and naively—this same tired framework has been picked up by some contemporary historians, even feminist ones.

In fact, masonic rituals always had great meaning. Biblical themes were popular in the eighteenth century, and mention was often made in newspapers and literature of biblical personages. Taking up such themes implied piety and seriousness about tradition, although not an unwillingness to tinker with old myths and symbols. But most important, rituals were expensive. Each carried with it the obligation of the candidate to fete the assembled, and all required new garments, insignia, and in some cases jewels for both men and women. Rituals carried status; they imitated aristocratic and church culture and at the same time were invented anew, intended to symbolize merit, not inherited or apostolic rights. In the 1740s, when men's higher degrees and probably women's rituals as well were being formulated in the Scottish rite, biblical themes were among those chosen for the men's Scottish degrees.[21] How appropriate that they should also be chosen for the new women's ritual. As French masonic historian Alec Mellor observed, to have loaded women's ceremonies with building references would have seemed inappropriate. Biblical references were also much more compatible with eighteenth-century French men and women trained on the Catholic catechism.[22]

Yet the very difference in the usage given these symbols in the adoptive lodges signals their distinctive pertinence to women. As their use expanded during the decades of adoptive masonry, the women themselves became inseparably attached to biblical themes, elaborated on them, and refused to let them be changed. While few male masons would have considered the biblical ceremony equal to their own, it would be far-fetched and unrealistic to picture them cynically pulling out a meaningless ceremony to keep the women quiet. By the time of Clermont's ritual, male masons who favored the admission of women had invested a great deal of time, money, and personal prestige in sponsoring and supporting women's lodges. It is improbable that they would have invented frivolous ceremonies given the rancor they encountered from brothers who opposed women's admission. As one of them put it, "Our honor has been compromised. Women are going to be seated among us in our temples."[23]

However contentious, Clermont's ritual became the model for all later rituals in female masonry, although ceremonies in the lodges of adoption did not become standardized until the 1780s. During the 1770s the role awarded to women in rituals changed. In Clermont's ceremony men generally led the proceedings while acknowledging that their "fathers" had erred because they "feared the discord that your beauty would bring" into the lodges.[24] As we just saw, in rituals established around 1775, women not only played a greater part in the ceremony, but in addition the lodge was not considered properly constituted without both the master and mistress present. All sisters voted, and the third degree contained an entire section devoted to the mistake masons had made in failing to admit women to membership in the past: "the cause can only be attributed to the ignorance of the time." The Grand Master then explained, "The possibility of reuniting the two sexes in our lodges was reserved solely for the happy days that we illuminate. Light is finally introduced into spaces that were occupied by shadows; our deep studies in the art of masonry have helped us find the true means of perfecting our edifices; it is through the help of our sisters who brought with them a heart that encloses the five columns of our order."[25]

The culmination of ritual evolution in the masonic lodges came in 1779 with the publication of *La vraie maçonnerie d'adoption* by Louis Guillemain de Saint Victor, a general and somewhat obscure writer of the era. This ritual became the most popular of all; Guillemain de Saint Victor seems to have created it from the most common adoptive ceremonies of the day. Throughout his 1779 edition are footnotes referring to practices in what he called "loges irrégulières," indicating, by inference, that his work represented the adoptive majority's actual, and perhaps not yet officially recognized, practices.

Like the earlier rituals, the 1779 ritual provides a window into the structural position of women in the masonic polity. They had made giant strides. The Grand Master still presided over the ceremonies as was required of all lodges under masonic law, but now the ritual was actually conducted by the Sisters Inspectress, Treasurer, and Introductress. The brothers who were their counterparts "assisted them, being present only to help them for the most part."[26] Even Grand Mistress, which had been an honorary position, became one of some substance by 1779. Furthermore, during the ritual for the first degree, the orator referred to the lodges of adoption as "our society of sisters," showing the growth of the organization from a male-sponsored, male-run organization dependent totally on the men's lodge to a women's organization run by and for women.[27] Even the ritual itself shows signs of having been combed for unconsciously disrespectful references to women. Gone were older references to women's curiosity, and in the catechism of the third degree, as the sign was being explained, the Grand Master told the candidate that touching the eye also referred to the male gaze; it meant "a mason . . . should look at his sisters only with the eyes of the soul, which means that he must respect their wisdom and their virtue."[28]

If Guillemain de Saint Victor's ritual was the culmination of the evolution of adoption's four basic degrees, the real explosion in women's visibility and leadership in the lodges manifested itself in two higher degrees dating from the last quarter of the century. They were known as Sublime Ecossaise and Amazonnerie Anglaise, and they introduced into lodge ritual a woman-centered celebration, a full-blown sense of self that would later be called feminism.[29]

In both higher degrees, women dominated the ritual and the symbolism. In Sublime Ecossaise—for the first time—a woman was the central figure in the narrative, entering the lodge holding a death head that was the signal for all brothers and sisters to stand. In the catechism for the degree, the candidate took the part of Judith, Jewish wife of the tribe of Simeon and a military figure in her own right. The Recipiendaire, as the biblical Judith, murdered King Nebuchadnezzar's general, Holophernes, and thereby saved the city of Bethulia. She did so, she said, for the "liberty of all my brothers and sisters." When asked by the Grand Priest what she wanted, she commanded that her followers and "all the people pray for me for five days."[30]

Even more remarkable was the higher degree of Amazonnerie Anglaise. How many women actually attained this degree is not known, but the existence of several copies of the ritual indicates it was not unique to one or two lodges. A significant number of unusual features in this ritual show women definitively in new positions in the leadership of the lodge. The rites by which women were initiated into this degree do not fit even remotely into the description of "male-determined judgments of virtue, merit and beauty" offered by one feminist historian.[31] The principal figure, as in Sublime Ecossaise, was a woman, the Queen of the Amazons. She ran the ceremonies, despite masonic law requiring the Grand Master to lead all adoption rituals. The Queen initiated both men and women, and her female officers had military titles and all the feminine charm of army drill sergeants. Throughout the ritual they shouted out commands to the other brothers and sisters. The catechism, where laws and beliefs of the degree were stated, called on women to recognize the injustice of men, to throw off the masculine yoke, to dominate in marriage, and to claim equal wealth with men, among other things.[32]

In one version of the Amazonnerie Anglaise ritual, the Grand Mistress (renamed the Queen) officiates, holds the constitutions, and queries her brother, the Grand Patriarch: What is the most important order of business for the day? How do men keep women under them? With these questions posed, she urges her sisters to be courageous, to cast off the bondage imposed by men, and to regard those men who refuse to obey their orders as tyrants. Now follows a discussion of how it is that men assert their dominance over women. Recognizing the growing importance of scientific knowledge, the answer prescribed in the ritual asserts that male dominance is built on the dignity conferred "by the study of the sciences" as well as "by the duties of the state and by the maintenance of arms."[33] Hence the second law of the Amazons requires that the sisters maintain arms and that they also study the sciences. Among these women the message of the French Enlightenment about the need for more scientific education has been applied to the search for equality; science will promote equality between the Amazons and the Patriarchs.[34] The educative ideals found among women freemasons of the 1780s look toward new, utilitarian forms of female sociability, ones that emphasize widespread educational reform. The 1795 salon of Madame Helvétius, who like her husband had been a freemason before the revolution, became a center for educational re-

In the engraving, inscriptions read: "R.G. Rehart del." and "S. Fokke fecit." The plinth bears the words "SILENTIO ET FIDE."

FIGURE 16. Frontispiece to *Almanach des Francs-Maçons: Pour l'année 1786* (The Hague, 1786), showing an allegorical figure, a woman with a rose and blindfold. Below is the motto of the Grand Lodge of the Netherlands, Silence and Faith. With permission of the masonic library, Prins Frederik Cultural Masonic Center, The Hague; copyright Grand East of the Netherlands.

formers like Sophie Condorcet, widow of the *philosophe*.[35] Might we
not legitimately speculate that the Amazons of the 1780s prepared the
way for these new, more modern forms of female sociability and educational idealism? At the very least the growing visibility of women
within the masonic movement may have something to do with the use
of female figures to reflect the highest ideals of the order.

Predictably, the women in the adoptive lodges of the 1780s knew
that the men who joined with them or supported their activities were
different. As a women orator in Dijon put it: "We have found just men
who, instead of offering us condescension . . . pride, and superiority,
present us with an association, a sharing."[36] These same sentiments are
expressed repeatedly in verse and song. The literature of adoption also
came to include explicit critiques of male arrogance written by men in
support of the women's lodges.[37] Where the Parisian *salonnières* were
sometimes at the mercy of their *philosophes*, or at the best of times
the ambitions of both coincided,[38] no less artfully hundreds of women
freemasons were taking a different route.

Again the rituals mark the way. In 1779, for instance, the prestigious
Loge des Neuf- Soeurs in Paris held an initiation ceremony at its lodge
of adoption. The brothers of the lodge—among them literati or admir-
ers of Franklin and Voltaire who had been personally honored by the
lodge—wrote a special ritual for women's initiation. Its words were
philosophical, filled with references to ancient Greece, Rome, and the
Near East; it was probably a masterpiece of its time. The women hated
it. In effect, they said, "These discourses have displeased us, tired us
out, even bored us." The epigoni of the *philosophes* were forced to return
to the ritual of Guillemain de Saint Victor. The displeasure of their
sisters was so pervasive that the brothers of the lodge were ultimately
required to explain their audacity in changing the ritual.[39]

In general, the rituals give only clues, not complete pictures; they are
small windows rather than doors to the life in eighteenth-century
lodges of adoption. The ritual symbols changed from the half builder,
half Old Testament symbols shared with male freemasonry to the Old

Testament symbols that were unique to the lodges of adoption. Then they moved on to uniquely feminist language. More significant, there was a growing respect for the position of women and a strengthening of their roles in lodge ritual, mirroring the manner in which their roles had grown in the structural, leadership side of the lodges.

Besides what they show about the changes in women's lodges, the rituals also reveal a seriousness of purpose. Citing a few superficial or outdated secondary sources, some feminist scholarship sees in the rituals little more than a farce, a means by which masonic men continued their hold over women. In fact, far from being a frivolous pastime, the women's masonic ritual provided their own rite of passage into the culture of Enlightenment. It gave women masons a share in the century's intellectual, secular, and civic life, just as the *salonnières'* philosophical musings won them a place in enlightened society. Beginning with the deism implicit in the evocation of the Grand Architect and ending with new social ideals of liberty, equality, and fraternity, the lodges could work as powerfully on an individual as any clandestine manuscript or polite gathering that entertained the heretical.

Enlightenment preoccupations appear in rituals, in masonic songs, in the private libraries of the women masons, and in the discourses in the lodges. The audacity and heterodoxy of the radical *philosophes* were not as commonplace as in the men's lodges—and they were by no means typical there[40]—but adoptive freemasonry offered a chance for women to experience and shape the new culture in ways meaningful to them. The first three degree rituals demonstrated friendship between individuals, the ideal of fraternity.[41] While some controversy surrounds the origin of the term *fraternity* as it was found in the revolutionary slogan, Liberty, Equality, and Fraternity, there can be little doubt that the fraternal concept was a strong element in all masonic lodges. Fraternity implied mutual aid, support, and trust among brethren. As Eric Hobsbawm has rightly observed, there was a strong emotional content in fraternity, "uniting something like the sentiments of kinship, friendship and love in the heightened atmosphere of something like religion."[42] The presence of this force in male lodges has been recognized for some time. The fact that it was also an extremely important aspect of female lodges has been generally overlooked. In both male and female lodges, the term *friendship* was used more frequently than the term *fraternity*, but the fraternal concept was clearly present. The ideal in adoptive freemasonry was "disinterested friendship" between women but also between men and women.[43]

Adoption lodge initiation rituals were perfectly formulated to steep the group's consciousness in this sense of virtuous friendship. Whether the design occurred through someone's specialized knowledge or happy accident, the rituals of adoptive masonry fit exactly the classic pattern of the tribal rites of passage, religious celebrations, and consciousness-raising seminars found around the world in many places and many times. In this classic pattern, a mentally open and prepared candidate first meditated in seclusion, often preparing psychologically for the death of her persona and rebirth into a higher consciousness. During the second part, the more public ceremony, she was given knowledge new to her through words, symbols, and her own active role-playing. Finally, with all tests passed, all knowledge acquired, and all oaths taken, she was introduced formally as a full-fledged member of the group and took her place with the others. If we doubt the impact that these ceremonies could have on women of the eighteenth century, we need only know that both women and men freemasons thought it dangerous for pregnant women to experience these ritual initiations.[44]

THE PUBLIC FACE OF VIRTUE

As she mastered the knowledge of the first three degrees, the masonic candidate learned how to be a virtuous friend. Women, whose earlier sense of friendship was often stunted by society and usually limited to family members, had an especially strong need to experience this new and individualizing concept. Spiritual unity, a pure and rare friendship, became a reality to the brother and sister masons, as their songs and discourses indicate. "Friendship among the common people is nothing more than a shadow, a disguise,' went the elitist words to one song in a 1775 collection. "Among us it is a sentiment, as solid as it is sincere."[45] In another song of the same collection, the sisters and brothers intone, "Here when we are together there is no sweeter pleasure; it is friendship that brings us together, all-consuming in our wishes."[46] The customary song for closing all adoptive lodges restated the ideal: "Let us join together hand in hand, let us stay together; let us give thanks to the fate of the bond that brings us together; to all the virtues open our hearts as we close this lodge."[47] Out of the friendship and fraternity found in the sociability of the meritorious, other virtues with implications for the organization of public life inevitably followed. "Liberty" and "equality" were words consistently interwoven with the fraternal ideal, and rituals such as the fourth, or Maçonne Parfait, degree reinforced both concepts and drew out their social implications. The setting, theme, and symbolism centered on the escape of the Israelites from bondage. The words employed throughout spoke of leaving bondage, of learning freedom through masonic instruction, of the unworthiness of the strong who enslave the weak, of the need for complete liberty through full commitment. The symbols included the ritual removal of a white iron chain from the candidate's hands and the symbolic release of a bird from captivity. Similarly, a series of words and symbols infused the degree ritual with the concept of equality. The Grand Master identified himself as only the first among equals; the candidate spoke of the lodge members as equal in everything but the wisdom imparted by degrees, and the songs of the lodge very often referred to this concept as basic to its life. Further, the brothers and sisters seemed to see their lodges as havens of equality where one could escape an unjust world. As a published song from the adoptive lodges put it: "La égalité / L'humanité / Voilà nos loix suprêmes."[48] In a reference to the princesses of the blood and their membership in the lodges, the secretary of La Candeur wrote in the *Esquisse des travaux* that the princesses came to the lodge to "enjoy among us this precious equality, the only happiness that they lack in the rank where fate has put them."

In "Essai sur le but d'Adoption" (also from *Esquisse des travaux)* the secretary observed that "the perfect equality that reigns among us is too widespread and too closely followed for any harm to come to our charming union?"[49]

By the 1760s both concepts, liberty and equality, appeared on the intellectual agenda of enlightened and reforming circles. To be sure, contradictions abounded. The message of liberty was somewhat confused in the adoptive rituals. As among *philosophes* and *salonnières*, the practice of equality in the lodges must have been highly qualified. Sister servants and princesses of the blood did not have remotely similar access to degrees. Yet, the Enlightenment experience lived through ritual could have its effect. The adoptive ceremonies helped bring women into the light of the century just as the intellectual discussions in the salons galvanized the zeal of the *salonnières*. Both were social experiences available only to the literate and the financially comfortable, but by the 1780s it had occurred to women who came out of one or the other social experience that larger, more egalitarian and practical reforms were now needed. Far from being the beginning of the end for feminist aspirations, the late Enlightenment brings to Western thought a new and more powerful feminist agenda.

By the last quarter of the century the adoptive lodges turned increasingly toward the utilitarian as well as toward domination by elite groups marginal to, or excluded from, the old nobility. Increasingly, the lodges were made up of a relatively new nobility at work in government service and jealous of its prerogatives. The members of many military lodges included nobles stationed in various parts of France, trying to set up a pleasant society in their outposts. In cities where there was a *parlement*, certain other lodges tended to serve as congregation points for government officials. It was these lodges, both judicial and military, that generally sponsored lodges of adoption. The judicial element, the new nobility of government service, became particularly strong in male and female masonry in the years after 1780, although its involvement in the organization began several years before that. In the male lodge La

Sincerité at Besançon, the 1778 *tableau* contained the names of forty-two brothers, of whom twenty-two held governmental positions.[50] La Sincerité had a lodge of adoption with twenty-five sisters, eight of whom are readily identifiable by their last names or titles as wives of government officials. Since most female masons were either wives or close relatives of lodge brothers, and since so many of the men had government-related positions, it is likely that more than eight women were members by birth of the *noblesse de robe*.

Dijon supported three men's lodges, one of which, La Concorde, was the gathering place for the judicial element. According to masonic historian Louis Amiable, from 1777 to 1783 the brothers included fifteen government officials and three military officers. A more recent study using a 1781 membership roster traced forty-one of forty-five masons from the lodge. Régine Robin found that twenty-two were members of the *Cours souveraines*, and there were eighteen *parlementaires*. Of the forty-one members she could trace, twenty-eight were nobles of the robe and thirteen were commoners.[51] If one compares the number found by Robin in Dijon in 1781 to the number of nobles of the robe in the Besançon lodge of 1778, there is a hint of the post-1780 growth in the judicial element in French freemasonry. Where just over half of the Besançon lodge brothers were nobles of the robe, the Dijon judicial membership stood at 62 percent.

Furthermore, in social orientation and economic level the commoners in the Dijon lodge seem closer to aristocracy than do most bourgeois. They were not merchants; true to the deep social divisions reflected in the lodges of most towns, merchants tended to belong to another lodge, Arts Reunis sous Saint Luc. The bourgeois members of La Concorde enjoyed independent means, generally living off land receipts.[52] Yet none of them could prove the four generations of nobility necessary to enter the Provincial Estates.

Significantly, La Concorde was the one lodge of the three in Dijon that sponsored a lodge of adoption. The Grand Mistress, the Grand Inspectress, and six others of a total of thirteen members were wives of government officials. Again, the remaining members may well have been close relatives of government officials, but since their names and titles did not identically match those on the male roster, the connection cannot easily be made. If extant records are any guide, women's masonry seems to have been particularly strong in Dijon and Besançon. Its strength may also have reflected the ideology and ambitions of elite social elements at odds with the privileges of yet older elites. Could bourgeois and *parlementaire* adoptive freemasonry in some sense have prepared the way for the subsequent strength of the republican clubs that emerged in exactly those cities in the early 1790s and about which Suzanne Desan has written?[53]

In Toulouse a similar pattern of government officials manifested itself, but with an interesting twist. Several lodges attracted barristers, but it was the partially aristocratic, partially government nobility lodge, de la Parfaite Amitié, that sponsored a lodge of adoption.[54] A roster of eighty-one members in 1786 listed thirty-eight government officials and twelve military officers. The nobility of the robe made up only 46 percent of the Toulouse lodge. However, while the membership of the men's lodge included both the older nobility of the sword and the newer nobility of the robe, in the lodge of adoption judicial wives predominated. Virtually all the highest offices of the lodge of adoption, also called de la Parfaite Amitié, were held by the wives of the judicial officials in the men's lodge.

The congregation of new, government-service nobility in the masonic lodges, and particularly their wives' activity in lodges of adoption, suggests that these ambitious women and men were building up a network of social connections and power within and between lodges; women freemasons sought to strengthen the authority of the *parlements* in their localities.[55] Particularly in the Toulouse lodge, there may have been strong social reasons for the two types of nobility to mix, and the wives may well have been part of an attempt by the nobility of the robe to grasp by association some of the elusive power held by the older nobility. It may also be that their exclusion from the upper nobility (because they fell one or two generations short of the required four) caused them to seek power and prestige behind the closed doors of a secret society. The masonic emphasis on merit and equality may also have been a means to deny the distinction between themselves and the upper nobility.

Some of the families in which the wives were active in a lodge of adoption evince an interest in the new, enlightened culture. At least half the books on the shelves of the Macheco family, for instance, three of whom were female masons, appealed to enlightened tastes: ancient literature such as works by Plutarch, Ovid, Virgil, Seneca, and Cicero, and contemporary works of Voltaire, Rousseau, and the English novelists.[56] These brothers and sisters in masonry may have found contemporary philosophy suitable to their needs and purposes. It expressed reformist impulses and gave them the sense of equality with the upper nobility they craved, while not directly depriving them of the prerogatives of the seigneurial world they enjoyed outside the lodges.

In the north of France, where many of the military lodges were located, there were large numbers of lodges of adoption. The women's lodges seemed to have great significance for the military. Perhaps the affective nuclear family, which developed in France largely in the nineteenth century, made an early appearance in these isolated military outposts, leading many military units to sponsor lodges of adoption. The better known of these lodges were those at Hesdin and Arras, near Boulogne and Nancy; those at Caen and Toul; and the lodge Les Bons Amis at Chinon, which moved with its regiment. As military units moved around the country, lodges of adoption seem to have been factored into the move. The lodge at Hesdin was originally peopled by the officers of the Royal Roussillon, but when the Regiment de Penthièvre-Dragon succeeded them, the male lodge and the lodge of adoption were both taken over completely by officers from the new regiment. The military lodge at Caen seems to have taken its lodges with it in a move to Nancy. Generally speaking, the officers of the regiment and their wives made up the bulk of the membership, but there were usually some local officials and their wives in the lodge as well.

Like the salons, then, the lodges of adoption may be presented as entry points to the organizing concepts of the Enlightenment. The lodges became "secret" places where women's power and merit grew and were expressed through elaborate ceremonies (many of them published), and where large numbers of women first expressed what we may legitimately describe as an early feminism. As one female orator in Dijon put her masonic pride and sense of self: "I will never think about [the lodge and its officers] without sensing a tenderness mixed with respect. [Like an artist faced with his masterpiece] at the height of an equally ardent ecstasy . . . I [will write], I, too, am a mason"[57] Not surprisingly, the lodges, like the salons, could have meaning for eighteenth-century French society as a whole. By the 1780s the tenor of the Enlightenment began to change from ideas to action, from philosophy to utility and philanthropy. If the *salonnières* and their *philosophes* were the intellectual leaders of the Enlightenment in philosophy, the women freemasons were leaders and models of the Enlightenment in philanthropy. Charity was at the heart of their work and their dogma.

The most powerful moment in the fourth-degree ceremony occurred when liberty, equality, and fraternity were linked through the concept of charity. The candidate released a bird from its cage, and it became a poignant example of the three ideas. Not only did the candidate hear the Grand Master tell her that liberty was a right of all God's creatures, but the orator also explained to her the mystery of the released bird. He said, "Madam, I await you at the Altar of Truth to teach you the greatest secret of the Masons and therefore the most inviolable secret . . . it is that the unhappy and unfortunate of the Earth are our friends, our companions, our brothers. They have a right to our favors. Might I hope that they will find in you a helpful friend, and would you like to give me proof of it?"[58] At this point, the orator held before the sister an offering platter, and if the sister put too much money on it, the orator gave it back to her, telling her, "Madam, we are convinced of your correct sentiments and will leave to you the right to put them into practice whenever you have the opportunity. May your generosity proceed from a heart as pure as the sacred fire you see on this altar?"[59]

Gradually charity became essential to the masonic experience. If free-masons did not genuinely see the poor as their equals, if they did not truly subscribe to the notion that God had created all creatures to be free, at least their charitable orientation was a product of some inner sense of public duty, no doubt formed at least in part by ritual indoctrination. Here is where the lodges again invoked the secular ideals commonplace in enlightened circles. As the elite Paris lodge, La Candeur, put it, charity was "of all our duties that which ought to have the greatest attraction for us, be it for the inner satisfaction it provides or for the public consideration that often follows it. It is not that we ought to be charitable for ostentation: no, my brothers and sisters, the greatest merit of a charitable act, after that of performing it well, is to keep it secret. The opportunity to do good is always under our feet; not to seize it is to discard happiness."[60] The happiness derived from charitable work is palpable in an oration given by Mme. de D—, the proud woman orator in Dijon. She loved her lodge and her sisters in part because, as she told them, "to the extent that you can, you console the afflicted, you help the miserable, you nourish the indigent. Even those who are not initiated into our mysteries are the recipients of your charity; and the special chain that links you to all your brothers also attaches you to the great chain of humanity, which links you to everything that exists."[61]

The charitable activities of women masons formed a bridge between their eighteenth-century club structure and their spiritual beliefs developed through secular lodge rituals. The most active years of the lodges of adoption were precisely the years when charitable activity at all levels was at a low point. In earlier times, people had responded to the misery of the poor because the French Counter-Reformation had stimulated a return to the traditional Christian duty of charity.[62] Such primarily religious motivation was common in the seventeenth century, and charitable activities reached their peak in the period from 1680 to 1760. After 1760 secularization led to fewer charitable donations in last wills and testaments; poverty had come to be seen as an economic problem, not an occasion for saving one's soul through almsgiving.[63] Thus, poverty moved onto the secular agenda as local societies sponsored essays and generally sought new ways of replacing structures that no longer functioned for the mass of the impoverished.

But at the same time the public began to repudiate traditional charity as the best way to care for the poor, poverty was spreading alarmingly. The growth in population, the increase in illegitimate births, and the rise in prices made the situation of the poor desperate. By 1790 about half the French population lived in poverty.[64] The crisis years were between 1760 and 1789. Private benefactors of the poor had declined in number, and the welfare state had not yet come to fill the vacuum. The work of freemasons, particularly the zealous women in their lodges of adoption, was critically needed. While masons and other private charitable groups could not hope to keep pace with the growing needs of the poor, they did help alleviate some of the suffering at a time when the traditional forms of charity no longer functioned.

At each lodge meeting a collection was taken up for the poor, and one officer was always assigned to the distribution of charity. This practice became commonplace in many men's lodges and in all French lodges of adoption. At times of special celebration, the poor were always remembered. To celebrate the birth of the queen's daughter in 1778, the brothers and sisters of the lodge La Sincerité in Besançon collected twelve *livres* from each member to buy wheat and distribute it as bread to the poor. The distribution was to be in the name of the freemasons but made through the offices of the priest of the Madeleine. Even when the priest objected to acknowledging the masons, "who are authorized neither by the King, nor by the law, nor by the State, nor by the Church," the brothers and sisters persisted.[65] They had individual bakers produce twelve hundred small loaves of bread that were distributed to the poor at the Hôtel de Ville by the mayor's staff.

With the birth of the dauphin in 1781, in addition to masses, Te Deums, and lodge festivities, the women embarked upon special benefit collections for the poor. Members of the Mère Loge, after mass at the church of Saint-Eustache, voted to pay for the education of all the poor male infants born the same day as the dauphin in the parish of Saint-Eustache.[66] The male and female lodges of La Colombe in Nevers took up a contribution in honor of the dauphin to clothe and feed twelve poor children and to give extra food to their families. Lodge members also sent clothing and a complete trousseau to a poor child who had been adopted earlier by the lodge and paid for his apprenticeship. At the same time the lodge La Concorde in Dijon distributed wheat to sixty poor families.[67]

The lodge La Candeur in Paris decided in 1778 on a plan for three acts of charity. Typical of other societies with a utilitarian, public outreach, they first sought to interest other masons and financed a gold medal prize for the mason whose essay could best answer the question "What method would be the most economical, the healthiest, and the most useful to society for raising foundlings from their birth to the age of seven?" The lodge wished to have the competitors focus particularly on the dangerous abuse by wet nurses who in large cities took in too many infants. Their second act of charity was to offer a gold medal to an academy charged with judging the usefulness to humanity of a charitable act. The third act consisted in a special collection to reward Vincent Bemin of the Regiment d'Anjou, who risked his life to save two children in Lyon the year before.[68]

These charitable activities were all part of an increasingly public posture assumed by the lodges. In the 1770s the Grand Lodge had sought to have a public presence in Paris, both to be near the government and to allay suspicions. By the 1780s, not only did the lodges of elite women in Paris contribute to various charitable projects, they also turned toward matters of state. La Candeur contributed cannons to the king's arsenal. Once freed from the yoke of religious superstition and initiated into the masonic mysteries, members of the women's lodge said that as freemasons and French women they had "the right to serve the State." With a gift to the king, a woman had become a "new Amazon who will join in the defense of the country."[69] Not surprisingly, the overtly political language found in adoptive masonry by 1782 moved another lodge of adoption to caution against freemasonry becoming *un corps politique*. It responded favorably to La Candeur's request for a donation but argued that "masonry is an order in the universe but not an order in the state."[70]

The political language echoing the Amazon imagery of adoptive ritual originated in the most royalist of women's lodges, but it was addressed to all the other lodges of adoption. The Paris lodge told its sisters throughout the masonic nation that every citizen approaches her prince with the confidence of being well received: "one forgets one's elevation . . . and both are made equal by their virtues."[71] Another women's ritual for 1791 claimed loyalty to the king but condemned the "cruel Nemroth, father and tyrant." Then the ritual song extolled the virtue acquired by meeting under the square and the compass but asked pointedly, "Que les Monarques de la terre / Ne prennent-ils de vos leçons?" (Do the monarchs of the earth ever learn your lessons?).[72]

Just as women's freemasonry evolved into more public functions, so public perceptions of the lodges changed as well. Throughout the middle decades of the century there were numerous plays intended for masonic as well as general audiences, and their content can well serve as a measure of attitudes toward female masons. As early as 1740—before there were lodges of adoption—*Les Fri-Maçons, hyperdrame* had all the well-rehearsed situations found in the women versus freemasonry antagonism, and it set the tone for other plays that used the same themes. In *Polichinelle, Maître Macon* of 1745, Mme. Catin, the overly curious wife of Brother Polichinelle, determined that she would discover the masonic secret and talked her three daughters into trying to wheedle it out of their lovers. In 1754 the comic play *Fra-Maçonnes* deviated little from the same weary themes of women's excessive curiosity and trickery. *Les françmacons*, emanating from Strasbourg in 1769, repeated the same themes.[73]

By the late 1770s and 1780s, when lodges of adoption had spread throughout France, such themes finally changed. In 1779, *L'Ecole de Francs-Maçons* depicted a young woman initiated into a lodge because of the compassion she showed for an unfortunate man. In 1786 a monologue found in *Polichinel*, which had now made its way to Rotterdam, asked, "Without the lodges of adoption, where would freemasonry be today?"[74] The text also recounted the fierce opposition that women's masonry had encountered in some lodges, but, significantly, it labeled the masonic detractor "brother puerile."

When in 1774 the Grand Orient in Paris voted to accept women, the response among male masons throughout western Europe either championed women or recorded angry protests. The lukewarm positions in between left few records. Grand Orator Brother Bacon de la Chevalerie, for instance, recalled for the assembled brethren the ancient mysteries of Isis and Osiris, the Greek sibyls, the Roman vestals, and the heroines of Christian Europe. He asked: "And why would the freemasons of France, who are fathers, husbands, sons, and brothers, not allow the most beautiful, the most interesting, the most sensitive half of the human race to participate in the order's spirit of equality and charity, which constitute the base of the moral principles of the Royal Art?"[75] But despite the encouraging orations coming from Paris, grumblings among masons about the admission of women kept recurring. A small book published in Amsterdam in 1779, *Recherches sur les initiations anciennes et modernes*, decried the action of the French masons as the beginning of decadence. In Paris, above all, the book claimed, admission of women would become a dangerous moral problem. The author, one M. L'Abbé R-, took direct issue with the reasoning of the supportive Parisian orator, Bacon de la Chevalerie, and advocated instead a gender segregation of ancient lineage: "Where did that French Orateur of M—get the idea that women were admitted to the mysteries of Isis and Osiris? Herodotus said expressly that they were never admitted to any Egyptian mysteries. The sybils were famous women prophets, not only in Greece but also in Rome; their virtue was greatly venerated there, as was that of the vestals; they lived in retreats far from the dealings of men: thus their example could not be given any weight in favor of the association of which he spoke."[76]A masonic text published in Geneva a few years later attacked the lodges of adoption as "a disastrous abuse."[77]

Despite these individual protests, the constitutional umbrella provided by the Grand Orient worked distinctively to foster the French adoptive lodges. That they should be mixed rather than wholly female is not unusual. There were no totally female formal organizations in eighteenth-century France. As Mellor observed, eighteenth-century society defined men as having a duty to protect women in public situations. To leave women alone in their lodges—however private they may seem to us—would have been considered desertion; probably the women themselves would have felt abandoned.[78]

Far from veering off the course set for elite women in France by the salons, women's lodges built on the foundation constructed by the *salonnières*; they broadened and deepened the experience of enlightened culture. The French evidence from the 1770s and 1780s suggests no masculinization of the public sphere and voluntary associations; rather, it falls into a general western European pattern: a turn toward the more democratic and utilitarian that boded ill for oligarchs and monarchs.[79]

Freemasonry exhibited protean characteristics throughout the eighteenth century. It could make a nobleman seem like one's brother when in fact nothing had changed in the larger society. It could give women a sense of equality when their daily lives at home displayed precious little of it. But the ability to dream, to imagine a different world, is arguably essential if social and political change will ever occur. Amid the secrets and rituals, a form of play with roots in the medieval guilds, the eighteenth-century lodges looked toward the modern, even if so many of their members preferred tradition and order of ancient lineage.

APPENDIX: FRENCH LODGES OF ADOPTION BY PLACE AND DATE

Annonay. The Loge de la Vraie Vertu was functioning in 1766 and was reconstituted by the Grand Orient in 1775.[80]

Arras. The Loge de l'Amitié was functioning in 1786, according to the Livre d'Architecture de l'Amitié.[81]

Bar-le-Duc. In 1787, Brother Nicolas Mazot complained about the formation of a lodge of adoption, but no lodge name was given.[82]

Beauvais. Problems were mentioned due to the lodge of adoption, but no date was given.[83]

Besançon. "Installation de la L . . . de la Sincérité a l'o . . . de Besançon avec un tableau de la L . . . et de la L . . . [sic] d'adoption. Registrée 22o 3246, 14 7ième 1778."[84]

Bordeaux. La Française Elue Ecossaise is mentioned in connection with the occurrence of a particular event there in 1775. La Loge l'Amitié is mentioned with regard to the installation of the Duchess de Chartres and several other noblewomen there in 1776.'[85]

Caen. A lodge of adoption was *souchée sur* (founded on) the Loge Saint Louis in 1785.[86]

Chinon. The lodge Les Bons Amis of the Mestre de Camp Générale de la Cavalerie was constituted in Chinon, but the lodge of adoption actually met in Nancy in 1787; a tableau exists).[87]

Confolens. The Loge de la Parfaite Union left a trace in the lodge dossier mentioning a date of 1786.[88]

Dieppe. La Félicité was attached to the mens loge Saint Louis, which was constituted in 1766. The women's lodge is thought to have existed that early also. Both lodges ceased functioning in 1773. La Félicité was reconstituted for the Regiment de Rohan-Soubise in 1782. In 1783 La Félicité inaugurated a new temple with the title Trois Coeurs Unis, which was the name of the men's lodge and was mentioned in a 1786 discourse by the Comtesse de Caumont. The next year, both lodges shortened their names to Coeurs Unis. The lodge Saint Louis du Regiment du Roi was here in 1775 when the infantry unit was stationed in the area.[89]

Dijon. The record of its 1783 founding can be found in "Tableau des soeurs qui composent la R adoption, sous le titre distinctif de la Concorde a l'orient de Dijon, pour l'année 5783."[90]

Dunkirk. The lodge La Parfaite Union du Regiment de la Mardi-Infanterie was here in 1781, according to a document in the library of Brother A. de Rosny.[91]

Hesdin (between Berck and Arras). In the *Journal du Boulonnais*, published from 1779 to 1790, the Abbot de Bazinghem related that in April 1781, a number of bourgeois women of the city were received with their husbands as masons in the lodge of adoption under the Loge de la Parfaite Union du Regiment de la Mark. La Félicité may be as old as the male lodge (1749) but was officially reconstituted by the Grand Loge de France in 1772. La Fidelité is mentioned as having received in membership La Marquise de Fléchin in 1782. The lodge of adoption of the loge Saint Louis à l'Orient du Regiment d'Infanterie du Roi is quoted directly 1 July 1786.[92]

Loches. A lodge there, la Ferveur Eclairée, apparently met at least once in 1777.[93]

Morlaix. The Loge la Noble Amitié is mentioned as existing in the year 1782.[94]

Nancy. One of the two lodges of adoption was *souchée sur* the lodge Saint Louis à l'Orient du Regiment d'Infanterie du Roi in 1785. There is a tableau dated 8 August 1787 for the Loge des Bons Amis."[95]

Nevers. There may have been a lodge of adoption affiliated with the lodge Saint-Jean de la Colombe as early as 1776."[96]

Paris. La Candeur is dated to 1775 by George Kloss. Kloss donated his library and vast masonic manuscript collection to the Grand Lodge in The Hague, and more evidence of French women's lodges may yet turn up in the Kloss collection. A 1778 letter to brothers regarding the sisters and correspondence between La Candeur (adoption) and the Grand Orient from 1778–79 are in the B.N. archives. Contrat Social has an event documented in 1780. La Fideité began as a male lodge and in 1777 was reconstituted by the Grand Orient. Dates of 1776–79 are given for Loge des Neufs-Soeurs by Loucelles, and a date of 1776 is given by Louis Lartigue. More information about this lodge has turned up in the masonic archives returned from Moscow.

In *Bulletin du bibliophile* is a *registre* containing the *procès-verbaux* of seances of the lodge of adoption Saint-Jean-de-la-Candeur from 21 March 1775, to 10 February 1785, and Marcy mentions a date of 1778 found in a *procès verbal de la 5 assemblée* of the lodge in the Archives Nationales. The Loge de Saint-Antoine is mentioned with names of members and a date of 1775, when the Duchess de Bourbon was installed as Grand Mistress of all French lodges at this lodge. There was also L'Unique Alliance in 1760. A judgment was made against the Venerable Master Fellon for having opened and held a session of a female masonic lodge.[97]

Rennes. A lodge of adoption (La Parfaite Union) existed here at least since 1774.[98]

Rochefort. The loge de l'Aimable Concorde is mentioned citing a problem the male lodge had in 1777; documentation was in the archive of the lodge Saint-Jean de Jerusalem in Nancy.[99]

Toul. A tableau dated 1786 is inscribed: "Tableau des freres et des soeurs qui composent la R . . . L . . . des Neuf-Soeurs a L'O . . . de Toul, de l'imprimerie de la loge, 1786."

Toulouse. At La Parfaite Amitié, the male lodge reconstituted by the Grand Orient in 1781, tableaus of the women's lodge exist for 1786 and 1787. The baptism of an infant and a marriage are mentioned elsewhere.[100]

Touraine. La Ferveur Eclairée is mentioned in a quote by Brother Saulguin, secretary of the loge des Coeurs Unis, after an installation ceremony in 1777.[101]

Valognes. The Loge de l'Union Militaire is mentioned with a date of 1786 and 1787. Loucelles gives the names of the members in 1787.[102]

Conclusion

If the ability to dream of a different social order was made possible by the eighteenth-century lodges, what can we say about their role in contemporary American society? In one sense I am less than qualified to comment, as I am not, nor have been, a freemason. But I do quite regularly address lodges in this country and abroad, and get asked by them to comment on their contemporary meaning. I also talk to brothers and sisters and learn something about their concerns. At present in the United States freemasonry is in serious decline, with numbers dwindling and lodges closing. Yet at the same time American reformers have arisen, many of them identified with what they see as the more liberal forms of freemasonry practiced in continental Europe. Central to their concerns are issues of gender and race.

Officially women are still not admitted as sisters in the American lodges. In fact, and in spite of the official position, lodges for women, and for men and women do exist in major cities and receive some encouragement from brothers who value gender inclusiveness. But this is a struggle, and the outcome is by no means certain. More lodges may close and charitable work cease before the inclusion of women becomes the official norm. In the meantime such exclusions seem increasingly beside the point, as slowly and only through struggle do masonic women appear closer to a still distant equality.

But there is another matter, that of race, perhaps even more serious in terms of its larger implications for American society in general. Vast numbers of lodges, particularly in the American South, are segregated rigidly by race. Recently when addressing an entirely white audience of freemasons in Louisiana—all without exception immensely gracious—I was asked what I thought about the future of the American lodges. What can be said in the face of an institutionalized social system that works against our highest civic ideals? I find it hard to imagine the young men and women of every imaginable racial background who populate my university classes—where an ease in social mixing is now the norm to be sought—being attracted to lodges that would exclude one or another of their friends. Obviously, the future does not lie with segregation.

This being said, there are hopeful signs. New publishing ventures are afoot and contemporary freemasons are taking a renewed interest in their historical origins. As Americans travel so too they see the alternative forms of freemasonry practiced elsewhere. The charitable commitment of the lodges remains strong—hospitals, homes for children, and the aged still receive generous masonic support. In Britain, France, and the Netherlands alliances are being formed between the lodges and centers for masonic scholarship located within major universities. This has not yet happened in the United States but it may come to pass.

But the historian is on relatively firm ground only when addressing the past. In the eighteenth century the lodges absorbed every aspect of the larger society: they craved the support of noblemen and elites; they saw women as different, or just plain inferior; they quarreled over status, rituals, imagined slights; and so on. In short their members were human in the way that Europeans were in the period. But there is more to the masonic story than the commonplace. The lodges exported on to the Continent an aspect of British social mores that pointed in a more egalitarian direction. The English displayed a "consciousness of rights."[1] As a result of the Revolution of 1688–89 they also enjoyed more rights and liberties than many of their Continental counterparts. Even in the Dutch Republic there was no habeas corpus, for example. Likewise in the British setting the aristocracy was not legally forbidden to engage in trade and commerce, as it was in France. Books were easier to publish in England than they were in France because censorship remained laxer throughout much of the period. Yet for all the freedoms enjoyed by some Westerners we must remember that the lodges spread with empire; they made it easier to live in India or the Caribbean. In some places they could be used to bond with local elites; in others they were just a part of an imperial social order where the superiority of Westerners was taken by them as a given. Yet in the nineteenth-century colonies, lodges could also sometimes be centers for reformers and nationalists. Whenever people meet in organized groups, over long periods, they acquire the ability to accentuate their desires, for good or for ill.

Meeting under *constitutions*—as the freemasons always called their rules and statutes—was first and foremost part of the constitutional monarchical tradition forged by the English civil wars, regicide, and social upheavals of the seventeenth century. At the present we take such rights and liberties for granted. There was nothing commonplace about them in the eighteenth century. The lodges naturalized constitutional practices, nationally organized and representative assemblies, voting and speaking before such assemblies. For these practices and habits opponents of the French Revolution blamed the freemasons, claiming that they conspired to cause it. In reality the lodges may be said to have pushed European mores, at least at home, ever so slightly in a democratic direction.

FURTHER READING

If you want to know more about freemasonry, many popular accounts exist. All should be used with extreme caution. Here I have chosen works where I know that the scholarship is reasonably sound. But so as not to tax the patience of readers, the list is also short and intended merely as a starting place.

Robert Beachy, "Club Culture and Social Authority: Freemasonry in Leipzig, 1741–1830," in Frank Trentmann, ed. *Paradoxes of Civil Society. New Perspectives on Modern German and British History* (New York: Berghahn Books, 2000).

Peter Clark, *British Clubs and Societies 1580–1800: The Origins of an Associational World* (Oxford: Clarendon Press, 2000). The book puts freemasonry into the larger social context of the time.

Mary Ann Clawson, *Constructing Brotherhood: Class, Gender and Fraternalism* (Princeton, N.J.: Princeton University Press, 1989). Now a classic in the field on the role of fraternalism in constructing masculine identity.

Jessica Harland-Jacobs, "All in the Family: Freemasonry and the British Empire in the Mid-Nineteenth Century," *Journal of British Studies* 42, 4 (October 2003): 448–82. This is an award winning essay and before long a good book by this author should follow.

Jessica Harland-Jacobs, "'Hands Across the Sea': The Masonic Network, British Imperialism, and the North Atlantic World," *Geographical Review* 89, 2 (April 1999): 237–53.

Arturo de Hoyos and S. Brent Morris, *Is It True What They Say About*

Freemasonry?: The Methods of Anti-Masons (Silver Spring, Md.: Masonic Information Center, 2004).

Margaret C. Jacob, *Living the Enlightenment: Freemasonry and Politics in Eighteenth Century Europe* (New York: Oxford University Press, 1991). Some of the arguments presented in the present book first appeared in this 1991 book, which contains extensive references in some cases not repeated.

Margaret C. Jacob, *The Radical Enlightenment: Pantheists, Freemasons, and Republicans*, second edition revised (Morristown, N.J.: Temple Books, 2003). This book first appeared in 1981; then in 2003 another historian, Jonathan Israel, borrowed its title. But his *Radical Enlightenment: Philosophy and the Making of Modernity, 1650–1750* (New York: Oxford University Press, 2003) left out the masonic side of the story; hence this revised and second edition.

Dorothy Ann Lipson, *Freemasonry in Federalist Connecticut 1789–1835* (Princeton, N.J.: Princeton University Press, 1977). This is an old book and hard to find, but a classic and about far more than the title suggests.

James Van Horn Melton, *The Rise of the Public in Enlightenment Europe* (Cambridge, Cambridge University Press, 2001). This is excellent background reading.

Helmut Reinalter, ed., *Freimaurer und Geheimbünde im 18. Jahrhundert im Mitteleuropa* (Frankfurt: Suhrkamp, 1983).

Marie-Cécile Révauger, "De la révolution américaine à la révolution française: Le Franc-Maçon dans la cité" in Élise Marienstras, ed., *L'Amérique et la France: deux révolutions* (Paris: Publications of the Sorbonne, 1990).

Jasper Ridley, *The Freemasons* (London: Constable, 1999). It has quite a few errors in small facts but is on the whole rational in its treatment of the myths surrounding masonic origins and practices. To be used with caution.

Douglas Smith, "Freemasonry and the Public in Eighteenth-Century Russia," *Eighteenth Century Studies* 29 (Fall 1995): 25–44.

David Stevenson, *The Origins of Freemasonry. Scotland's Century, 1590–1710*, Cambridge: Cambridge University Press, 1988.

Mark A. Tabbert, *American Freemasons. Three Centuries of Building Communities* (Lexington, Mass.: National Heritage Museum; New York: New York University Press, 2005). The book is intended for coffee tables but has some very useful images; it has a masonic origin.

Anton van de Sande and Joost Rosendaal, eds. *"Een stille leerschool van deugd en goede zeden": Vrijmetselarij in Nederland in de 18e en 19e eeuw* (Hilversum: Verloren, 1995). Essays on Dutch freemasonry; one in English and the basis for chapter 3 in the present book.

Maurice O. Wallace, *Constructing the Black Masculine: Identity and Ideality in African American Men's Literature and Culture, 1775–1995* (Durham N.C.: Duke University Press, 2002). Contains a fascinating chapter on Prince Hall freemasonry.

R. William Weisberger, Wallace McLeod, and S. Brent Morris, eds. *Freemasonry on Both Sides of the Atlantic*, East European Monographs (New York: Columbia University Press, 2002). There is a good essay here on the myths surrounding the masonic symbolism *not* present on the dollar bill; essays explore the history of the lodges in Mexico, the United States, and the British Isles.

NOTES

INTRODUCTION

1. Jasper Ridley, *The Freemasons* (London: Constable, 1999), chap. 2.

2. Steven C. Bullock, *Revolutionary Brotherhood: Freemasonry and the Transformation of the American Social Order, 1730–1840* (Chapel Hill: University of North Carolina Press, 1996). There are also good essays on the American side of the story in R. William Weisberger, Wallace McLeod, and S. Brent Morris, eds., *Freemasonry on Both Sides of the Atlantic* (Boulder, Colo.: European Monographs, distr. New York: Columbia University Press, 2002).

3. Robert D. Putnam, *Bowling Alone: The Collapse and Revival of American Community* (New York: Simon and Schuster, 2000), chap. 3.

4. See Theda Skocpol, *Diminished Democracy: From Membership to Management in American Civic Life* (Norman: University of Oklahoma Press, 2003). See also Joanna Brooks, "Colonization, Black Freemasonry, and the Rehabilitation of Africa," in Malini Johar Schueller and Edward Watts, eds., *Messy Beginnings: Postcoloniality and Early American Studies* (New Brunswick, N.J.: Rutgers University Press, 2003), 237–50; Theda Skocpol and Jennifer Oser, "Organization Despite Adversity. The Origins and Development of African American Fraternal Associations," *Social Science History* 28 (2004): 367–437. For the role of freemasonry in imperial imaginings, see Peter Merrington, "A Staggered Orientalism. The Cape-to-Cairo Imaginary," *Poetics Today* 22, 2 (2001): 323–64.

5. David Stevenson, *The Origins of Freemasonry: Scotland's Century, 1590–1710* (Cambridge: Cambridge University Press, 1988), and also his *The First Freemasons: Scotland's Early Lodges and Their Members* (Aberdeen: Aberdeen University Press, 1988). For French freemasonry see also the whole issue of the journal *L'Histoire* 256 (July–August 2001) and Pierre-Yves Beaurepaire (the author of many works on eighteenth-century freemasonry), *Nobles jeux de l'Arc et loges maçonniques dans la France des Lumières* (Paris: Editions Ivoire-Clair, 2002).

6. For a more detailed account see *L'Histoire*, 256. For a book that gathers up all the supposedly masonic symbolism associated with the founding of the American republic and presents it as truth see David Ovason, *The Secret Architecture of Our Nation's Capital: The Masons and the Building of Washington, D.C.* (New York, HarperCollins, 1999). And for a credulous account of the freemasons and the Knights Templar, see Christopher Knight and Robert Lomas, *The Second Messiah: Templars, the Turin Shroud and the Great Secret of Freemasonry* (London: Century, 1997).

7. For more on the text and its history, see http://www.adl.org/special_reports/protocols/protocols_intro.asp

CHAPTER 1. ORIGINS

1. For a more detailed account, see Margaret C. Jacob, *Living the Enlightenment: Freemasonry and Politics in Eighteenth Century Europe* (New York: Oxford University Press, 1991).

2. See Steven Epstein, *Wage Labor and Guilds in Medieval Europe* (Chapel Hill: University of North Carolina Press, 1991).

3. Anthony Black, *Guilds and Civil Society in European Political Thought from the Twelfth Century to the Present* (Ithaca, N.Y.: Cornell University Press, 1984), chaps. 5, 12.

4. See also Roger Dachez, *Des Maçons opératifs aux Francs-Maçons spéculatifs* (Paris: EDIMAF, 2002); John Hamill, *The Craft: A History of English Freemasonry* (Leighton Buzzard: Crucible, 1986); Douglas Knoop, G. P. Jones and Hamer Douglas, eds., *The Early Masonic Catechisms* (Manchester: Manchester University Press, 1943, 1963, 1975). For a meditation on the role of Newtonianism at the origins, see Alain Bauer, *Aux origines de la Franc-Maçonnerie: Isaac Newton et les newtoniens* (Paris: Dervy, 2003).

5. Some of the earlier evidence for Wren comes from a letter of 1774 from the masonic historian De Vignoles, in Kloss MSS, 190 E. 47, The Library of the Grand Lodge, The Hague, "Le Chev. Wren fameux architecte, intendant des Bâtimens du Roi, membre du Parlement, ayant été élu en 1710 pour la seconde fois G. M. des la Société; cf. J. S. M. Ward, *Freemasonry and the Ancient Gods* (London: Simpkin, Marshall, Hamilton, Kent, 1921), 159–60, citing a manuscript note in the Bodleian from John Aubrey, "This day [18 May 1681] is a great convention at St. Paul's Church of the fraternity of the free [free then crossed out and "accepted" put in its place] Masons, where Sir Christopher Wren is to be adopted a brother & Sir Henry Goodrie of ye Tower."

6. See [Anon.], *The Secret History of the Free-Masons: Being an Accidental Discovery, of the ceremonies Made Use of in the several Lodges . . .* , 2nd ed. (London, 1725), iii, prints a portion or version of the Old Charges with the references to Hermes.

7. Stanton J. Linden, ed., *The Alchemy Reader: From Hermes Trismegistus to Isaac Newton* (Cambridge: Cambridge University Press, 2003), 9, 191, 208.

8. David Stevenson, "Masonry, Symbolism and Ethics in the Life of Sir Robert Moray, FRS," *Proceedings of the Society of Antiquaries of Scotland* 114 (1984): 407–8; Elias Ashmole, *Memoirs of the Life of that Learned Antiquary . . . published by Charles Burman, Esq.* (London: 1717), 15.

9. See Jacob, *Living the Enlightenment*, 32–46, making use of the Archives and Record Center, Dundee, Scotland, MS Dundee Mason Trade, Lockit Book, 1659–1960, unfoliated, and MS GD/GRW/M 2/1.

10. David Stevenson, *The First Freemasons: Scotland's Early Lodges and Their Members* (Aberdeen: Aberdeen University Press, 1988).

11. Royal Society of London, MS Register Book (C)IX.

12. Royal Society of London, MS Register Book (C)IX.

13. British Library, MSS ADD 4295, ff.18–19, and the libertine text reads: Extrait des registres du Chapitre général des Chevaliers de la Jubilation, tenu à Gaillardin, Maison de l'ordre, le 24 9bre, 1710:

Nous, Les Chevaliers de la Jubilation, à tous ceux que ces presentes lettres verront, Salut, joye, santé, Pigeons, Poules, Poulardes, Chapons, Perdrix, Faisans, Bécasses, langues fourrées, Jambons; *Bonum vinum, et que semper bonum apetitum*, &c.

Savoir faisons qu'a la requête du Chevalier Böhm, Échanson de l'Ordre, nous nous serions joyeusement assemblez en chapitre Général, au tour d'une table, garnie d'un gros aloyau, *cum fricaceis et saladibus*; et qu'ayant mangé *cum summo judicio* et bu *ad modum egregie*, nous aurions écouté, avec toute l'attention que le bruit de nos crocs permette les Griefs du dit Échanson contre le Sr Jean Frédéric Gleditsch, Chevalier du dit Ordre, qu'il nous a dénoncé comme infracteur de nos très gaillardes & joyeuses *constitutions*, et comme le (1er) perturbateur de la bienheureuse tranquilité dont a toujours joui l'ordre jusques à présent, depuis sa première institution, disant,

Que ledit Chevalier *Jean Frédéric Gleditsch* s'étant engagé par un voeu solennel à observer perpétuellement les *statuts* et *règlemens* de notre ordre, qui sont d'être toujours gaillard, joyeux, content, pret à rire, à boire, a chanter, a danser, à jouer, à badiner, à folatrer, à batifoler, &c. et a vivre sans amour clandestin. . . .

It is signed by Prosper Marchand, among others. It appears in the appendix of Margaret C. Jacob, *The Radical Enlightenment: Pantheists, Freemasons, and Republicans*, 2nd ed. rev. (Morristown, N.J., Temple Books, 2003). For early masonic usage of the term "constitutions," see British Library, Sloane MS 3329, f. 142 referring to "Charges in ye Constitution."

14. Jacob, *Living the Enlightenment*, chap. 6.

15. Guildhall Library, London, MS 5992, dated 20 October 1677; cf Jacob, *Living the Enlightenment*, 241, nn. 77–80.

16. See Giuseppe Giarrizzo, *Massoneria e illuminismo nell'Europa del Settecento* (Venice: Marsilio, 1994); Jon Mee, "Millenarian Visions and Utopian Speculations," in Martin Fitzpatrick, Peter Jones, Christa Knellwolf and Iain McCalman, eds., *The Enlightenment World* (New York: Routledge, 2004), 541.

17. A. S. Frere, *Grand Lodge, 1717–1967* (Oxford: Oxford University Press, 1967). For the engraving see Bernard Picart, *Naauwkeurige Beschryving der uitwendige Godsdienst-Plichten, Kerk-Zeeden en Gewoontens van alle Volkeren der Weerelt* (Amsterdam: Hermanus Uytwerf, 1738), 233.

18. James Anderson, *The Constitutions of the Free-masons: containing the history, charges, regulations, & of that most ancient and right worshipful fraternity* (London: William Hunter, 1723).

19. Abbé de Vertot, *Histoire des Revolutions* (Paris: F. Barois, 1719), 12, 117.

20. British Library, MSS ADD 4295, ff. 18–19.

21. For easy access to a portion of the text, see Margaret C. Jacob, *The Enlightenment: A Brief History with Documents* (New York: Bedford, 2001).

22. British Library, MSS ADD 4295, f. 19 gives the following as signers: ~~G. Fritsch Grand Maître~~ (name crossed out), M. Bohm, Échanson de l'Ordre, G. Gleditsch Trésorier de l'Ordre, Ch. Le Vier, Arlequin et Bouffon de l'Ordre, Bernard Picart Barbouilleur et enlumineur de l'Ordre, de Bey Graveur du sceau de l'Ordre, P. Marchand, Secrétaire de l'Ordre.

23. University Library, Leiden, Marchand MS 2, dated 1756.

24. UL, Leiden, Rousset de Missy to Marchand, Marchand MS 2, f. 47, 28 February [1752]: "Savey vous que cela auroit été grand train vers le Pantheisme si ses Thèses eussent passé et en même temps les 10 énormes vol. De L'Encyclopédie . . ."

25. Hassan El Nouty, "Le panthéisme dans les lettres françaises au XVIII siècle: aperçus sur la fortune du mot et de la notion," *Revue des sciences hu-*

maines 27 (1960): 435–57; and see Jonathan Israel, *Radical Enlightenment: Philosophy and the Making of Modernity, 1650–1750* (Oxford: Oxford University Press, 2001), 610–12.

26. For the original text of Anderson's *Constitutions* (London, 1723), see http://www.2be1ask1.com/library/anderson.html#dieu.

27. See Jacob, *Living the Enlightenment*, inter alia.

28. [Anon.], *Le mal épidémique des Francs-Maçons* [1748]; a copy can be found in Margaret C. Jacob, ed., *Freemasonry: Early Sources on Microfiche, 1717–1870* (Leiden: Interdocumentation, #FVR-3.8/1). This is a rare text and the original is in the Library of the Grand Lodge, The Hague. For copies of those 1738 and 1751 condemnations see Georges Virebeau, *Les Papes et la Franc-Maçonnerie* (Paris: Documents et Témoignages, 1977), 15–20. For a copy, see http://freemasonry.bcy.ca/anti-masonry/papal/in_eminenti.html. The archives in the matter have been richly exploited by José Antonio Ferrer-Benimeli, *Les archives secrètes du Vatican et la franc-maçonnerie*, 2nd French ed. (Paris: Dervy, 2002), 136 ff.

29. "Livre de Constitution," Library of the Grand Lodge, The Hague.

30. Archives of Bien Aimée, Library of the Grand Lodge, The Hague, brievenarchief, no. 80, dated 24 June 1757; for a description of the meeting; see Jacob, *Living the Enlightenment*, 125–26.

31. See the Waldegrave MSS, Chewton Mendip, Somerset; cited by the kind permission of Lord and Lady Waldegrave.

32. Archives générales, Brussels, MS 1105 A 124, Conseil privé, 1786, and MS A 124, 1104.

33. Library of the Grand Lodge, The Hague, Kloss MS 190E47.

34. Library of the Grand Lodge, The Hague, MSS de Vignoles; also Kloss MSS 190.E.47.

35. Archives of Bien Aimée, Library of the Grand Lodge, The Hague, Visitors' Book.

36. For Ramsay's oration see G. M. van Veen, "Andrew Michael Ramsay," *Thoth* 28, 2 (1977): 27–28 (a publication of the Grand Lodge of the Netherlands); for a copy of the oration on the web see http://www.srmason-sj.org/web/heredom-files/volume1/andrew-michael-ramsay.ht mo n; and for the jewelry, see Archives générales, Brussels MS 1105 A 124.

37. *Statuts de l'Ordre Royal de la Franc-Maçonnerie en France* (1773).

38. Bibliothèque municipale, Grenoble, MS Q 50.

39. Bibliothèque nationale, Paris, MS FM 4 76, ff. 36–41.

CHAPTER 2. DAILY LIVES AS MEASURED IN MASONIC TIME

1. Nathaniel Ames, *An Astronomical Diary, or an Almanack* (Boston, 1729), without pagination.

2. For one such, see Margaret Jacob and Matthew Kadane, "Missing Now Found in the Eighteenth Century: Weber's Protestant Capitalist," *American Historical Review* 108 (February 2003): 20–49.

3. For this early history and a listing of many, but not all French almanacs from the period see John Grand-Carteret, *Les almanachs français: Bibliographie—Iconographie . . . 1600–1895* (Geneva: Slatkine Reprints, 1968).

4. Cecil Adams, "The Freemasons' Pocket Companions of the 18th Century," *Ars Quatuor Coronatorum* 45 (1935): 165–231.

5. *Almanach oder Taschen-Buch für die Brüder Freymäurer der vereinigten Deutschen Logen* (1776); copy found in the Library of Freemasons' Hall, Philadelphia.

6. Nehemiah Strong (late Prof. of Mathematicks and Natural Philosophy in Yale College), *An Astronomical Diary, Kalender or Almanack* (Hartford, Conn., 1790), same for 1807.

7. Hosea Stafford, *Stafford's Almanac . . . 1779* (New Haven, Conn.), back cover.

8. Andrew Agnecheek, Philom. *The Universal American Almanack, or Yearly Magazine, For the Year of our Lord 1764; and from the Creation, according to Prophane History, 5713.* I am grateful for the opportunity to consult this rare text in the Library of Freemasons' Hall, Philadelphia. An incomplete almanac of 1799 could be by the same printer as the 1764 one; see A 22 Pen 99; it gives stamp duties, the meeting of courts and Quakers but contains nothing masonic.

9. Maurice O. Wallace, *Constructing the Black Masculine: Identity and Ideality in African American Men's Literature and Culture, 1775–1995* (Durham, N.C.: Duke University Press, 2002): 64.

10. *The Masonic Almanac and Pocket Companion . . . 1801* (Philadelphia: Printed by John Bioren), 44.

11. *Masonic and Citizens' Annual Almanac for the AM 5814, A.D. 1814* (Philadelphia: Thomas De Silver).

12. See, for example, Thomas Harbin, *The Traveller's Companion: Containing Variety of Useful yet Pleasant Matters Relating to Commerce and Converse . . . Digested in a portable Volume, for the opportunity of Implying all vacant and leisure hours* (London, 1702). See John Gadbury, *Ephemeris; or A diary*

astronomical, astrological, meteorological . . . (London, 1719), for a calendar that begins with the creation of the world in 5658, Noah's Flood in 4012, Christ baptized in 30, and so on. For a similar set of dates, see also Richard Saunders, *Apollo Anglicanus* . . . (London, 1745).

13. In the Masonic Library in The Hague; see *Nederlandsche Vrymetzelaars Almanach* (1793). American black freemasons said that Solomon had been black; see Wallace, *Constructing*, 68.

14. For physico-theology see Hosea Stafford, *Stafford's Almanac* . . . *1778* (New Haven, Conn.); same for 1779, which does give the estimated population for all the European countries.

15. Henry Coley, student in the mathematicks and the celestial science, *Merlinus Anglicus junior, or The starry messenger, for the year of our redemption* (London: M. Read, 1745).

16. *Almanach des francs-maçons* . . . *1788* (The Hague: R. van Laak, 1788), 35–37.

17. *Nederlandsche Vry-Metzelaars Almanach, voor het Jaar 1793* (Rotterdam, C.R. Hake, 1793), 49.

18. Tycho Wing, Philomath, *Olympia domata or, An almanack for the year of our Lord God, 1745* (London: T. Parker, for the Company of Stationers, 1745).

19. John Gadbury, *Ephemeris; or, A diary astronomical, astrological, meteorological, for the year of our Lord, 1719* (London: For the Company of Stationers, 1719).

20. Gadbury, *Ephemeris*. Cf. Jonathan Dove, *Dove: Speculum anni: or, an almanack for the year of our Lord God, 1709* (London: J. Heptinstall, for the Company of Stationers, 1709), and published for a decade or more beginning in at least 1701; and *Astrologus Britannicus: or an almanack for the year of our redemption, 1707, . . . By Richard Gibson, . . .* (London: Thomas Wilmer, for the Company of Stationers, 1707). The author identified himself as an astrologer; in addition *An Almanack for the year of our Lord God MDCXXVIII . . . Calculated by John Godsmith* (London, 1728), which gives the astrological charts for all months.

21. Nathaniel Ames, *An Astronomical Diary, or an Almanack* . . . *1762* (Boston, 1762), often without pagination.

22. *The family almanack, for the year of our Lord 1749. . . . To which is added, a physical directory, . . .* By Nathanael Culpepper (London: G. Woodfall, for the Company of Stationers, [1749]). From earlier in the century, see *The En-*

glish chapman's and traveller's almanack for the year of Christ, 1707. . . . (London: Tho. James, for the Company of Stationers, 1707).

23. *The gentleman's diary, or The mathematical repository*. . . . *The fifth almanack ever publish'd of this kind* (London, 1745); *The ladies Diary; or, The woman's Almanack, for the year of our Lord, 1745* (London, 1745).

24. *Nieuwe volledige en nuttige altoosdurende societeit Almanak* (Amsterdam: Baalde, 1761) gives the history of the Franco-Prussian War complete with engravings of battle scenes, as well as masonic ceremonies; also supplies a list of the kings of Europe.

25. *The Free-Masons' Calendar: or, an Almanac, For the Year of Christ 1775* . . . *containing* . . . *Many useful and curious Particulars relating to Masonry* (London, 1775), 17.

26. Ibid., 18.

27. Ibid.

28. On Wren as a freemason, see Lisa Jardine, *On a Grander Scale: The Outstanding Life of Sir Christopher Wren* (New York, HarperCollins, 2002), 448–50.

29. *Almanach des francs-maçons: Pour l'Annee commune 1778* (Amsterdam: Jean Schreuder, 1778).

30. Note that in a diary of 1793 (note 17) there is a category, "Regeeringe der Maan in des Menschen Lighaam," the governance of the moon over human bodies; from the Library of the Grand Lodge, The Hague.

31. J. Rixey Ruffin, "'Urania's Dusky Vails': Heliocentrism in Colonial Almanacs, 1700–1735," *New England Quarterly* 70, 2 (June 1997): 306–13.

32. *Almanach des francs-maçons* . . . *1787* (The Hague: R. van Laak, 1787), "Discours d'un orateur," 29–35.

33. *Almanach des francs-maçons* . . . *1787*, "Oraison funebre Prononcée par le T.V. Frère D.P. le 27 "Aout 1786. Dans la Loge La Perséverance à l'Orient de Maestricht," 43–43.

34. *Almanach des francs-maçons. Pour* . . . *1785* (The Hague: R. van Laak, 1785), 29–31.

35. *De Almanach der vrye metzelaaren voor het jaar 1781* (Amsteldam (sic), 1781).

36. *Nederlandsche Vrijmetzelaars Almanach* (Rotterdam, 1793).

37. *Almanach des francs-massons. Pour l'année bissextile 1772*; on the back page Jean Schreuder is listed as the publisher and the engraved symbol of the famous Amsterdam lodge, La Bien Aimée is on the inside page; see pp. 24–25

for the list. This imperial theme is explored to great effect by Jessica Harland-Jacobs, "All in the Family: Freemasonry and the British Empire in the Mid-Nineteenth Century," *Journal of British Studies* 42 (2003): 448–82.

38. *Almanach des francs-maçons: Pour l'Année commune 1779* (The Hague: R. Van Laak, 1779).

39. See Margaret C. Jacob, *Living the Enlightenment: Freemasonry and Politics in Eighteenth-Century Europe* (New York: Oxford University Press, 1991), 139.

40. *Almanach des francs-maçons . . . 1779* (The Hague: R. Van Laak, 1779).

41. *Almanach des francs-maçons . . . 1763* (Amsterdam: Chez la Veuve de Jean François Jolly, 1763), songs provided in the final pages, unnumbered, complete with musical notation.

42. *Almanach des francs-maçons . . . 1781* (The Hague: R. Van Laak, 1781), 31.

43. Ibid., 23.

44. *Almanach des francs-maçons . . . 1787*, 28.

45. Nathanael Low, *An Astronomical Diary; or Almanack . . .* (Boston, 1770); same title for 1774 and discussing "measures arbitrary and repressive."

46. *Almanach des francs-maçons . . . 1777* (Amsterdam: Jean Schreuder, 1777), 21.

47. *Almanach des francs-maçons . . . 1778* (Amsterdam: Jean Schreuder, 1778), 17.

48. *Almanach des francs-maçons . . . 1763*, 42–43.

49. *Almanach des francs-maçons. Pour l'Année commune 1787* (The Hague: R. van Laak, 1787), p. 35.

50. *Almanach des francs-maçons . . . 1776* (n.p.: Imprimé pour l'usage des frères, 1776).

51. *Almanach des francs-maçons . . . 1782* (The Hague: R. van Laak, 1782), 24–25.

52. *Almanach des francs-massons. Pour . . . 1768* (n.p.: Imprimé pour l'usage des frères), 1768, 42–43. The oration here being quoted was by Jean Schreuder in Amsterdam, a brother in the lodge of Rousset de Missy. For attachment to the state see *Almanach des francs-massons . . .1772* (n.p.: Imprimé pour l'usage des frères), 18–19. For the discussion of social virtues see *Almanach des francs-massons . . . 1773* (n.p.: Imprimé pour l'usage des frères), 46–47, with an emphasis on the lodges in Germany. Sometimes the French accents do not appear on these title pages.

53. *Almanach des francs-massons . . . 1772* (n.p.: Imprimé pour l'usage des frères), 17.

54. Same series of almanacs as above, but for 1775, 29–30.

55. *Almanach des francs-maçons . . . 1777* (Amsterdam: chez Jean Schreuder, 1777), 22.

56. *Almanach des francs-maçons . . . 1781* (The Hague: R. van Laak, 1781), 29.

57. *Almanach des francs-maçons . . . 1788*, 32.

58. *Almanach des francs-maçons . . . 1787*, 31.

CHAPTER 3. SCHOOLS OF GOVERNMENT

1. On the concept of a "constitution," see Graham Maddow, "Constitution," in Terence Ball, James Farr, and Russell L Hanson, eds., *Political Innovation and Conceptual Change* (Cambridge: Cambridge University Press, 1989).

2. The Library of the Grand Lodge, The Hague, MS 41:9, f. 62, dating from 1780–81.

3. *Almanach des francs-maçons: Pour l'Année commune 1781* (The Hague: R. van Laak, 1781), "Discours prononcé en Grande Loge Nationale le 19 Mars 1780 par le Ven. Mtre de la Loge présidiale l'Indissoluble," 25.

4. On the anti-Jesuit nature of German lodges, see W. Daniel Wilson, *Unterirdische Gänge: Goethe, Freimaurerei und Politik* (Berlin: Wallstein, 1999). For a different perspective, see Joachim Bauer and Gerhard Müller, *"Des Maurers Wandeln, es gleicht dem Leben": Tempelmaurerei, Aufklärung und Politik im klassischen Weimar* (Rudolstadt: Hain Verlag, 2000).

5. Wayne A. Huss, *The Master Builders: A History of the Grand Lodge of Free and Accepted Masons of Pennsylvania*, vol. 1, *1731–1873* (Philadelphia: Grand Lodge of Pennsylvania, 1986), 20.

6. Douglas Smith, *Working the Rough Stone: Freemasonry and Society in Eighteenth-Century Russia* (DeKalb: Northern Illinois University Press, 1999), 50.

7. For documentation in the French case, taken from records at the Archives nationales, Marine B2 317, dated 1742, on officers of the Marine in Brest, see Pierre Chevallier, *Le sceptre, la crosse et l'équerre: sous Louis XV et Louis XVI, 1725–1789* (Paris: Honoré Champion, 1996), 288–89.

8. For those records, see Archives générales du Royaume, 3 rue de Ruysbroeck, Brussels, MS A 124 1104, "confréries supprimés," 1786–87. See also

Nicholas Till, *Mozart and the Enlightenment* (New York: W.W. Norton, 1992), 189–95.

9. Archives générales, Brussels, MS II05 A 124, Conseil privé, 1786. "Le sousigné chargé de la part de la Grand Loge National de la Monarchie Autrichienne établi à Vienne, de veiller à l'execution des Edits de Sa Majesté émanés le 9 Jan. & I May 1786 relativement aux affaires maçonnique de la Province des Pays-Bas Autrichiens."

10. Archives générales, Brussels, MS 1105 A 124, Conseil privé.

11. *Reedevoering uitgesprooken door een Broeder Orateur in eene wettige Loge op St. Jan's Dag, den 27 December 1755*, printed but not published, 6–7.

12. Margaret C. Jacob, *Living the Enlightenment: Freemasonry and Politics in Eighteenth Century Europe* (New York: Oxford University Press, 1991), 85, quoting from Kloss MS at the Library of the Grand Lodge in The Hague, MS 190 E 47.

13. Jürgen Habermas, *The Structural Transformation of the Public Sphere: An Inquiry into a Category of Bourgeois Society* (1962; Cambridge, Mass.: MIT Press, 1989), 35.

14. José Antonio Ferrer-Benimeli, *Les archives secrètes du Vatican et la francmaçonnerie* (Paris: Dervy, 2002): 157–72, 586–88, 603–619.

15. Archives of La Bien Aimée, Brieven archief, no. 50, letter of Baron deBoetzelaer, 7 January 1757; the Library of the Grand Lodge, The Hague.

16. For a facsimile copy of the oration, see G. van Veen, "Andrew Michael Ramsay," *Thoth* 28, 2 (1977): 27–57 (a publication of the Grand Lodge of the Netherlands).

17. Archives générales, Brussels, MS 1105 A 124; a document entitled "Francs-Maçons et jeux de hazard" and dated 1766. In a letter of 7 August 1770, from Neny to Crumpipen, we learn that the engraver, Castille, was a Jew who has now left the country.

18. Bibliothèque nationale (hereafter B.N.), Paris, MS FM 4 76, a collection of Scottish rite rituals, all from the second half of the century, see ff.36–41. Note that a lodge in Montpellier adopted for their master "the man more versed in the sciences and physical speculations." See B.N. FM 2 3* 9, 24 June 1782.

19. Royal Society of London, MS Register Book (C) IX, ff. 240–52, also discussed in Marsha Keith Schuchard, *Restoring the Temple of Vision: Cabalistic Freemasonry and Stuart Culture* (Boston: E.J. Brill, 2002), 576–78.

20. Royal Society of London, MS Register Book (C) IX, ff. 240–52.

21. It is discussed in detail in Margaret C. Jacob, *The Radical Enlightenment: Pantheists, Freemasons and Republicans*, 2nd ed. rev. (Morristown, N.J.: Temple Books, 2003).

22. For this letter and many examples of the parallels between masonic governance and the practices of the state, from the Library of the Grand Lodge, see MS 41:48 (2), 24 December 1769; MS 41:48 14 April 1771. For the comment about "free and independent," see MS 41:48 (2), 19 August 1770; MS 41:48 (2), 19 August 1770; MS 41:48 14 April 1771; MS 41:48, 19 May 1782; MS 41.48 (2), 6 June 1779.

23. For a discussion of these moments see Jacob, *Living the Enlightenment*, chap. 7.

24. The Library of the Grand Lodge, The Hague, MS 41:48 14 April 1771.

25. MS 41:48, 19 May 1782.

26. MS 41:48 (2), 6 June 1779.

27. Letter dated Amsterdam, February, 1778 from Le Comte de Leca Istria, Capitaine Corse, Brievenarchief, no. 288; the Library of the Grand Lodge, The Hague.

28. [Anon.], *Redevoering over het gedrag der Vry-Metselaaren, Jegens den Staat* (Amsterdam, 1752), 29; located in University Library, Amsterdam, Redev. D.32. Publication listed at end of tract as Amsterdam, "By P. H. Charlois," 1752.

29. François Furet, *Interpreting the French Revolution*, trans. Elborg Forster (New York: Cambridge University Press, 1981), 197.

30. Pierre Chanu, preface to André Delaporte, *L'idée d'égalité en France au XVIII siècle* (Paris: Presses universitaires de France, 1987), xi.

31. Lynn Hunt, *Politics, Culture, and Class in the French Revolution* (Berkeley: University of California Press, 1984), 199.

32. See also James McClellan, III, *Colonialism and Science: Saint Domingue in the Old Regime* (Baltimore: Johns Hopkins University Press, 1992). In this island colony by 1789, 3,000 whites presided over 500,000 slaves and one in three white men were freemasons.

CHAPTER 4. MONEY, EQUALITY, AND FRATERNITY:
FREEMASONS NEGOTIATE THE MARKET

1. *Statuts et réglemens particuliers, de la R. L. des A. R. . . . a l'O[rient] de Paris, 5774* [1774], 72.

2. Quoted from one of the earliest extant continental books of constitutions, modeled on the *Constitutions* (London, 1723); Archives du département de la Côte d'Or, Dijon, MS Livre des Constitutions et Reglemens Generaux des Francs et Reçus Maçons en particulier pour La Loge de Lausanne. Aprouvés par tous les Frères, 3 December 1741.

3. Chambre de commerce et d'industrie, Marseille, no. 132, printed but anonymous, *Essai sur les causes de la Cherté de l'argent . . . à Marseille* (Nîmes, 1774), 27, "It must be the case that the Capitalist has . . . a very powerful motive for engaging in commerce . . . that is a strong self-interest."

4. Bibliothèque nationale (hereafter B.N.), Paris, MS FM 1 136, 1785–1809, ff. 393–486, *demandes de secours*, for an entire collection of these letters. I quote from them at random.

5. B. N., MS FM 1 136, ff. 393–486; letters asking for charity; and f. 511 et seq. records of monthly, even weekly, payments; f. 426, f. 431; ibid., f. 420, letter from one Joseph Schwartzmann, originally Danish.

6. Ibid., f. 486, dated Paris, 6 June 1791.

7. Ibid., f. 484, thirteenth day of the tenth month, 5790 [1790], signed Fr. Bernard De Lamarguisie.

8. Ibid., f. 466, Paris, fifteenth day of fourth month, 5789 [1789], signed De la Salle.

9. *Almanach des Francs-Maçons, Pour l'Année commune 1779* (The Hague: R. van Laak, 1779), 25.

10. The Library of the Grand Lodge, records of Bien Aimée, MS 41, Notulen, ff. 46–47; on the fees, ff. 62–63. Cf. Brievenarchief, no.103, "Project on the harmony of elections in this lodge."

11. Ibid., f. 66, on replacing beans with money, 14 March 1760.

12. The Library of the Grand Lodge, The Hague, MS 38.1: "Notulen der Vergaderingen van . . . Concordia Vincit Animos, van den 13 Juli 1755 tot en met 30 Augustus 1761," written entirely in French although Dutch was also spoken in the lodge. This lodge met in Amsterdam and had in it many men of French origin, among them, and for a time its orator, the abbé Claude Yvon, author of major articles in Diderot's *Encyclopédie* (1751) and one of his confidants. In trouble with the censors he fled to Amsterdam in 1752.

13. The Library of the Grand Lodge, The Hague, MS 41:48 (2), December 26, 1767: "zeekere Missive, van den Broeder Ryk van Vliet, geweezene Meester van de Agtbare Loge De Goede Trouw te Utrecht, ann deeze Nationale Groote Loge geaddrescert, behelzende het verhaal van een meenigte ram-

pspoeden en noodlottige gevallen, denzelve overkomen, waar door tot dat uiterste was gebragt, om onderstand," and minutes of the lodge, La Bien Aimée, MS 41:8, f. 86, February 26, 1772; and again, f. 123, "arme, oude of ongelukkige zeelieden."

14. [Anon.], *Essai sur les Mysteres et le veritable objet des Franc-Maçons*, 2nd ed. (Amsterdam, 1776), found at B.N., Res. II 2326 (2, i–v); 18–19: "Men are not equal, neither by power, talents, or physique. Each has a terrible and natural inclination to want to dominate the other . . . thus is would be impossible to render all individuals perfectly equal. The equality of freemasons consists in regarding all as brothers and giving a reciprocal duty of comfort and charity. Good morals are founded on such an equality and Christian charity has the same principle at its base. All good political administration rests on a moral system."

15. Library of the Grand Lodge, The Hague, MS 41–42b, cf. 148a/158a154, 11 January 1760.

16. *Un siècle de Franc-Maçonnerie dans nos régions 1740–1840* (Brussels: Galérie CGER, 1983), 182; notes by Hugo de Shampheleire.

17. Bibliothèque nationale et universitaire, Strasbourg, MS 5437, régistre des procès-verbaux de la Candeur, 1763–76, f. 25, 1763: "Le Venerable proposed to augment the price of the reception of an apprentice and *un compagnon* that had been fixed at four louis or 86, and to put them at 120 livres and six livres for servants."

18. Bristol Record Office, MS 20535(291), f. 4; five shillings to be paid by each member, each quarter; two guineas plus a sum "for clothing," i.e., gloves and other items of regalia, upon admission.

19. Library of the Grand Lodge, The Hague, MS 23.1 Kast 158. B, f. 115. The past master of a lodge in Middleburg speaks in French to the new master and his brothers: "Accept the public vote that you have accomplished with the tender care of a father, the application of a true freemason, a zeal capable of giving an example to all brothers, and fraternal love for our August order and its propagation in our province." The orator continues: "Receive the public evidence that you have perfectly achieved all the duties of this important charge [that of holding an election]."

20. Jürgen Habermas, *The Structural Transformation of the Public Sphere: An Inquiry into a Category of Bourgeois Society*, trans. Thomas Burger with Frederick Lawrence (Cambridge, Mass.: MIT Press, 1989), 50–52. German edition first published 1962.

21. Ibid. 35.

22. Bibliothèque arsenal, MS 11556, f. 347, the spy Dadvenel writing on 5 February 1746: this is Danguy, "the widow who resides with Le venerable, or the Master of the lodge, a carpenter . . . a negro who holds a place among the trumpeters of the royal guard."

23. Abbé Barrel, *Mémoires pour servir* a *l'histoire du Jacobinisme* (London, 1797), 2: 262. For the influence of the book, see Emily Lorraine de Montluzin, *The Anti-Jacobins, 1798–1800* (New York: St. Martin's Press, 1988).

24. Michael Roberts, "Liberté, Egalité, Fraternité: Sources and Development of a Slogan," *Tijdschrift voor de Studie van de Verlichting* 4, 3–4 (1976) 329–69.

25. François Furet, *Interpreting the French Revolution*, trans. Elborg Forster (New York: Cambridge University Press, 1981), 179.

26. Clarence Crane Brinton, *The Jacobins: An Essay in the New History* (New York: Russell and Russell, 1961), 14. See also Pierre Lamarque, *Les francs maçons aux Etats Généraux de 1789 et a l'Assemblée Nationale* (Paris: EDIMAT, 1981), 6–7. Two hundred of the deputies and 37 of the supplementary deputies (of a total of 1,165 members and substitute deputies) were freemasons.

27. B.N., Paris, FM 1.111, ff. 401–5, concerning the request for constitutional status from the lodge in Strasbourg, La Candeur, 10 January 1763; f. 405, 26 September 1763: "Nous vous adressons aussi le tableau de notre loge, vous y verrez que la loge de la Candeur ne reçoit que des frères de Nom et d'un Etat honnete, ils ont été etonnés d'apprendre que le frere Litzelmann [the actor] etoit membre de la grande loge." He could come to their lodge as a visitor but never as a member.

28. B.N., Paris, MS FM2. 426, ff. 28–30; in this instance the Grand Lodge is also questioning the probity of the orator of the lodge, who is an actor; f. 143, letters of 1778. Archives municipales, Strasbourg, Boite 35/9 Compte Général, 1783–84, for the lodge St. Genevieve [the one being questioned for its high number of merchants]. Prices were as follows: 60 to 72 livres for reception as an apprentice; monthly fees 1.1–10; grade of Elu, 1.36; reception as master, 1.24, etc. In 1784 the lodge received 1,129, paid out 808 livres, and had in reserve 1,339. Cf. Ph. Claus, "Un centre de diffusion des 'Lumières' à Strasbourg: La Librairie Académique (1783–99)," *Revue d'Alsace* 108 (1982): 81–102, and Bertrand Diringer, *Franc-Maçonnerie et société a Strasbourg au xviiième siècle*, Mémoire de Maitrise (Strasbourg: Université des

sciences humaines de Strasbourg, 1980). There were 1,500 masons in the 1780s in this town of 50,000; 10,000 in Paris (population more than 500,000).

29. Library of the Grand Lodge, MS 41:42b, 15 October 1760.

30. This example is drawn from my *Living the Enlightenment: Freemasonry and Politics in Eighteenth Century Europe* (New York: Oxford University Press, 1991), chap. 1.

31. David Stevenson, *The First Freemasons: Scotland's Early Lodges and Their Members* (Aberdeen: Aberdeen University Press, 1988); and by the same author, *The Origins of Freemasonry* (Cambridge: Cambridge University Press, 1988).

32. For what follows, see Alex. J. Warden, ed., *Burgh Laws of Dundee with the History, Statutes and Proceedings of the Guild of Merchants and Fraternities of Craftsmen* (London: Longmans, Green, 1872), 167, for 1697–99; 186, 177, 193–94. On the role of the craft guilds, see Anthony Black, *Guilds and Civil Society in European Political Thought from the Twelfth Century to the Present* (Ithaca, N.Y.: Cornell University Press, 1984), 43. See also the comments of Daniel Mornet on the way in which freemasonry was imbedded in the French ancien régime; Daniel Mornet, *Les origines intellectuelles de la révolution française (1715–1787)* (Paris: Cohn, 1933), 375–87.

33. Warden, *Burgh Laws of Dundee*, 193–94.

34. Ibid., 262–63.

35. Archive and Record Centre, Dundee, MS GD/GRW/M 2/1, entry dated May 3, 1711, "from James Cox in part of his freedom, 16:13:4." Total income for that year appears to have been forty-nine pounds. Pounds Scots should be divided by twelve for the equivalent pounds sterling. In the late seventeenth century, skilled masons could be paid three and a half to five pounds Scots per week. For a description of the Dundee lodge, see Stevenson, *The First Freemasons*, 94–97.

36. William Mackay Mackenzie, *The Scottish Burghs* (Edinburgh: Oliver and Boyd, 1949), 69, citing a charter of 1364 for the older language. Occasionally "freedom" and "liberty" were used interchangeably in the sixteenth century (135). Note that women were regularly admitted as burgesses (140). Cf. Stevenson, *The First Freemasons*, 97. One version of the *Constitutions*, now extremely rare, *The Old Constitutions Belonging to the Ancient and Honourable Society of Free and Accepted Masons* (London: J. Roberts, 1722), 16–17, encouraged workers to protect their wages and labor and absolutely forbade a mason from taking over the work of another.

37. See on this process Erie Wehrli, Jr., "Scottish Politics in the Age of Walpole" (Ph.D. dissertation, University of Chicago, 1983), 10–11.

38. James Thomson, *The History of Dundee* (Dundee: Durham and Son, 1874), 134.

39. Dundee, *Charters, Writs and Public Documents of the Royal Burgh of Dundee, 1292–1880* (Dundee, 1880), 147–49. For the workhouse, see Warden, *Burgh Laws*, 190–91 also on famine in the vicinity. See Thomson, *History of Dundee*, 119. There is little correlation between the names of known Jacobites in 1745 and the membership lists of the freemasons, yet note that the name of one Thomas Blair, merchant, can be found in both. David Allen, "Political Clubs in Restoration London," *Historical Journal* 19 (1976): 561–80. The association of freemasonry with Whiggery was continued by the Tories; see Simon Robertson Vasey, "The Craftsman, 1726–1752: An Historical and Critical Account" (Ph.D. dissertation, Cambridge University, 1976), 58, 184 ff. Cf. Linda J. Colley, "The Loyal Brotherhood and the Cocoa Tree: The London Organization of the Tory Party, 1727–1760," *Historical Journal* 20 (1977): 77–95. Clerk to the Mason Trade, Dundee Mason Trade, Lockit Book, 1659–1960, unfoliated but dated nearly annually from 1659. For similar language, see Harry Carr, *Lodge Mother Kilwinning, No. 0: A Study of the Earliest Minute Books, 1642 to 1842* (London: Quatuor Coronati Lodge, 1961), 27–28; yet see also 34 and 186, where the term "elected" is used in 1645 and henceforth appears intermittently and is synonymous with "chosen." Its usage began to take on the modern meaning in the 1670s as gentry started to take office in the lodge. Cf. Dundee Mason Trade, Register of entries of Masters and Journeymen, 1659–1779, MS GD/GRW/M311, 28 December 1667. For the right to confer those privileges, see the records of the Register of Deeds of the Burgh of Dundee, vol. 26, 903–5, dated 1659, printed in *Ars Quatuor Coronatorum* 99 (1986): 194–95.

40. See Clerk to the Mason Trade, Dundee Mason Trade, MS Locket Book, 1659–1960, unfoliated, but dated nearly annually from 1659; see also Dundee Mason Trade, Register of entries of Masters and Journeymen, 1659–1779, MS GD/GRW/M3/1, 28 December 1667.

41. See MS Locket Book, for those years.

42. See MS Locket Book, 27 December 1734.

43. Grand Lodge of the Netherlands, archive of La Bien Aimée, B.A. 6, f. 11, dated 11 April 1756, from Rousset de Missy: "The letter for our institution was from the Venerable Linslager, master of the lodge in Leeuwarden, who had been received by a Scottish permission."

44. Dundee Mason Trade, Sederunt Book, 1736–1807, 27 December 1737.

45. Lockit Book, f. 1; cited by Stevenson, *The First Freemasons*, 197, as Inventory 13.1.

46. Black, *Guilds and Civil Society*, 43. See also the comments of Daniel Mornet on the way in which freemasonry was imbedded in the French ancien régime, in *Les Origines intellectuelles*, pp. 375–87, and see also Heather Swanson, "The Illusion of Economic Structure: Craft Guilds in Late Medieval English Towns," *Past and Present* 121 (November 1988): 39.

CHAPTER 5. WOMEN IN THE LODGES

1. François Furet, *Interpreting the French Revolution*, trans. Elborg Forster (Cambridge: Cambridge University Press, 1981). Taking the Furet approach is Ran Halévi, *Les loges maçonniques dans la France d'Ancien Régime* (Paris: A. Colin, 1984), which is quite different from the approach taken in Margaret C. Jacob, *Living the Enlightenment: Freemasonry and Politics in Eighteenth-Century Europe* (New York: Oxford University Press, 1991).

2. Library of the Grand Orient, Paris (from the Moscow collection) MS 113.2.96, 6 February 1746.

3. See Jacob, *Living the Enlightenment*, chap. 5

4. Grand Orient, MS 113.2.96, Le 6 Fevr.1746. Le f. . . . dénonce au R. Atel des Loges de Franche Maçonnes ditte des Soeurs de l'Adoption, qui se tiennent en ville; La Loge décide dans san sagesse de prévenir."

5. Metropolitan Museum of New York, Prints Room, no. 61.621.5, *Sun Foundry*, Glasgow, n.d. but from early in the nineteenth century, p. 379, for text and engraved pictures which promised that the lavatories were "chaste in style."

6. Bibliothèque nationale, Paris (hereafter B.N.), FM 4 1249, no place or date but clearly from the late eighteenth century and entitled "Statutes des dames."

7. "Soeur Dupont ayant été adoptée a la Loge des Parfaits Elus depuis l'année 1757 a l'honneur de représenter a ses freres et soeurs sa situation actuelle, ayant engage ses effets par une maladie qu'elle a essuyée. Elle ôse se flatter que ses freres et soeurs lui porteront un secours d'humanité. La jour de son adoption, on lui présente un coeur qui fut le seul garant de leur amitie" (Soeur Dupont, undated, B.N, FM 1136, f. 431). The record of her lodge appears to have been lost. This request for charity was a routine one, made by

both male and female members, as well as widows. While this letter is un-dated, all the letters in the file date from the 1780s, with one or two as late as 1792. On early quasi-masonic and French-speaking organizations for men and women, which may have evolved into lodges of adoption, see *La Franc-Maçonne ou revelation des mysteres des Francs-Maçons. Par Madame *** (Brus-sels, 1744; Leiden, n.d.), IDC microfiche, p. 12; "ces loges hermaphrodites" are mentioned. See also *L'Ordre Hermaphrodite ou Les Secrets de la sublime Felicité . . . Au Jardin d'Eden* (Paris, 1748; Leiden: IDC microfiche collection, 1985), 14–15, where it is argued that the order replicates the Garden of Eden; *Formulaire du cérémonial en usage dans l'ordre de la felicité. Observe dans chaque Grade* (n.p., [1745]; Leiden, 1985), microfiche. These tracks are on microfiche from IDC, 151 Hogewoord, Leiden, Netherlands, in a collection edited by Margaret Jacob.

8. By the late 1780s, French freemasons were aware of this unique integra-tion; see *La Maçonnerie Ecossoise comparée avec les trois professions et le Secret des Templiers du 14 siècle*, pt. 2, *Orient de Londres* (1788), 72: "Les françois ont même voulu une maçonnerie pour les femmes; et malgré les Supérieurs Incon-nus [a secret Jesuit form of freemasonry supposedly descended from the Stu-arts and their allies] ils ont créé une maçonnerie pour les femmes." This tract provides interesting background for the twists and turns of pre-1789 clerical-masonic hostility and the myths each side generated.

9. See Jacob, *Living the Enlightenment*, chap. 5. Part of the ritual is repro-duced in Margaret C. Jacob, "Freemasonry, Women, and the Paradox of the Enlightenment," in Margaret Hunt, Margaret Jacob, Phyllis Mack, and Ruth Perry, eds., *Women and the Enlightenment* (Binghamton, N.Y.: Institute for Research in History, Haworth Press, 1984). Some of the ritual can be seen in *Chansons de l'Ordre de L'Adoption ou la maçonnerie des femmes. . . . Avec un Discours préliminaire sur l'Establissement de l'ordre, prononcé le jour de l'ouver-ture, & de la constitution de la Grande Loge a la Haye, Au temple de l'Union, May 1751, a la Haye* (Leiden, IDC microfiles n.d.). A copy survives in the B.N. and in The Hague, and the microfiche collection available from IDC.

10. "Recueil et Collection de toutes les instructions de la maçonnerie en tous grades. A l'usage du frère Bassand. Suite l'Adoption des soeurs. Le chan-tier des fendeurs, L'Ordre de la felicité," B.N. MS FM 4 148, ff. 303–8; for Lot, see ff. 320–27. Clermont is mentioned on the title page. It is worth noting here that in the 1740s French male lodges had been suspected of "sod-omy"; see Jacob, *Living the Enlightenment*, 183. Such suspicions were not,

however, unique to France; they were also commonplace in the Netherlands and were occasionally documented in Britain.

11. *L'Adoption ou la Maçonnerie des Femmes a La Fidelité* (The Hague, [1775]), 25. A similar ritual appears in MS 2110, Bibliothèque de Bordeaux. Here too the men lead but also proclaim "a perfect equality between all Masons."

12. The ritual is in a book entitled *Livre contenent tous les grades de Ia veritable maçonnerie*, B.N, FM 4 79. The title of the ritual, unchanged in the original, was "Maçonnerie des dames ou la Maçonne d'adoption par le Prince de Clermont grand Maître de Orient de France deduis en quatres grades."

13. *L'Adoption ou la Maçonnerie des Femmes a La Fidelité*, 26, 13, 41. In these sentiments the lodges may also have been reflecting their sensitivity to charges of sodomy. In another work, the garden imagery is mixed with other female symbols used to represent the four parts of the world (B.N. FM 4 149, ff. 167–71).

14. *Manière de conferer la maçonnerie d'adoption au beau sexe suivant l'usage de Ia loge de L'Inalterable Amitié* (1784), B.N. 8 Fac-Sim 411. For lodges decorated as the Garden of Eden, see B.N. FM 4 149, ff. 167–68.

15. This is contained in a discourse by a brother addressed to his sisters (B.N. FM 4 148, ff. 303–8). Clermont is mentioned on the title page of this manuscript collection.

16. André Doré, "La Maçonnerie des dames: essai sur les grades et les rituels des loges d'adoption, 1745–1945," *Bulletin du Grand College de Rites* 96 (1981): 14–15.

17. See Jacob, *Living the Enlightenment*, chap. 8.

18. See the archives of Montpellier, B.N. FM 113. In a letter of 3 December 1787, the Grand Lodge is fighting with a new lodge in the town about its not having followed procedures for consulting with other lodges before applying for a constitution; in a letter dated 7 June 1784, a lodge has raised objections to the formation of a new lodge because the brothers have never heard of the men on its list; 21 December 1778, a lodge's constitution is declared null and void; in 1784 the Grand Lodge is arguing that it has always treated every lodge equally, etc. (B.N. MS FM 1 87). On quarreling in Bordeaux, see B.N. FM 1 86, from 1783; on the same in Calais, see B.N. FM 1 86, from 1786–87. For how masonic language in Montpellier could be adopted to revolutionary purposes, see J. A. Chaptal, *Catéchisme a l'usage des bons patriotes* (Montpellier, 1790), 12–13; Chaptal, the chemist, was quite active in the lodges before 1789.

19. *La Loge Rouge devoilée*, new ed. (July 1790), B.N. Baylot Impr. 1108. The Bibliothèque historique de la ville de Paris has a 1789 edition. The title page of both tracts is done in red. For the circles capable of writing such a tract, see Amos Hofman, "The Origins of the Theory of the *Philosophe* Conspiracy," *French History* 2, 2 (1988): 152–72. My thanks to D. M. McMahon for calling attention to this essay.

20. See *Hommage maçonnique de la mere loge écossaise d'adoption, A la Sérénissime Soeur Marie-Thérèse-Louise de Carignan, Princesse de Lamballe, sa Grande Maitress; . . . Par le Frère Robineau de Bëaunoir* (Hérédon, 1781); a copy can be found in the Library of the Grand Lodge, The Hague, and is available in microfiche from IDC.

21. Henri-Felix Marcy, *Essai sur l'origine de Ia Franc-Maçonnerie et l'histoire du grand Orient de France* (Paris: Foyer Philosophique, 1956), 1: 134.

22. Alec Mellor, *Les grandes problèmes de la Franc-maçonnerie* (Paris: Belfond, 1976), 113–14.

23. Alphonse Aulard. "Notes de lecture, féminisme et franc-maçonnerie à Confolens sous Louis XVI," *La Revolution française* 12 (July-September 1921): 257.

24. MS 2110, Bibliothèque de Bordeaux.

25. *L'Adoption ou la Maçonnerie des femmes en trois grades* (The Hague, 1775), 44. The argument is notably similar to the one used in the 1751 songbook associated with the Loge de Juste, *Chansons*. Compare the undated "Statuts de dames," which records how lodge meetings cannot be held without the master and mistress present, and that all brothers and sisters "ont le droit de voter" (B.N. FM 4 1249).

26. [Louis Guillemain de Saint Victor], *La vraie maçonnerie d'adoption* (London, 1779), 21. There were multiple editions of this work in the 1780s.

27. Ibid., 42.

28. Ibid., 107.

29. A more extensive analysis of these two degrees can be found in Janet M. Burke, "Through Friendship to Feminism: The Growth in Self-Awareness Among Eighteenth-Century Women Freemasons," *Proceedings of the Annual Meeting of the Western Society for French History* 14 (1987): 192–93.

30. "Adoption Grade de Sublime Ecossaise," Kloss Collection, no. 44, 10, Library of the Grand Lodge, The Hague.

31. As argued by Dena Goodman in *The Republic of Letters: A Cultural History of the French Enlightenment* (Ithaca, N.Y.: Cornell University Press, 1994) 102.

32. "Adoption. Amazonnerie Anglaise ou Ordre des Amazonnes," Kloss Collection, no. 44, 15, Library of the Grand Lodge, The Hague.

33. These details are contained in a collection of Scottish-rite rituals, all dating from the second half of the century; see B.N. MS FM 4 76, ff. 36–41. Note the growing emphasis on science in some lodges of the period. A lodge in Montpellier adopted for its master "the man more versed in the sciences and physical speculations" (see B.N. FM 2 309, dated 24 June 1782).

34. On this phase of the Enlightenment, see Bruno Belhoste, "Les caractères généraux de l'enseignement secondaire scientifique de la fin de l'Ancien Régime à la Premiere Guerre mondiale," *Histoire de l'éducation* 41 (1989): 8–9. For an attempt to counter women's lack of access to science, see Charles J. de Villers, *Journées physiques* (Lyon, 1761).

35. R. R. Palmer, *The Improvement of Humanity: Education and the French Revolution* (Princeton, N.J.: Princeton University Press, 1985), 223–26. As Palmer points out, there remained elitist elements in these salons just as there had been in the lodges and salons of the eighteenth century. Goodman states that a *salonnière* "in her journal . . . could study and improve herself rather than society" (*Republic of Letters*, 81). For evidence for actual reforms, particularly in science education, see the reports sent in by teachers in Archives nationales, Paris, F17 1344/1, ff. 12–36, from the year 6.

36. "Discours prononcé par Madame de D . . . 25 January 1782," MS 1415, Bibliothèque municipale, Dijon.

37. [Un Chevalier de tous des Ordres Maçonniques], *La Vraie Maçonnerie d'Adoption dédiée aux dames* (Philadelphia [a false imprint], 1783); Leiden, microfiche, pp. 14–17. Available from IDC.

38. See Dena Goodman, "Enlightenment Salons," *Eighteenth Century Studies* 22, 3 (1989): 339–40.

39. Dixmerie, *Mémoire pour la Loge des Neuf-Soeurs* (n.p., 1779), 21–23. New records on this lodge have returned to the Grand Orient from the Moscow archives.

40. See Margaret C. Jacob, *The Radical Enlightenment: Pantheists, Freemasons, and Republicans*, 2nd ed. rev.(Morristown, N.J., Temple Books, 2003).

41. A comprehensive treatment of Enlightenment concepts in ritual can be found in Burke, "Through Friendship to Feminism," 188–89, 194–95.

42. Eric J. Hobsbawm, "Fraternity," *New Society* 27 (November 1975): 472. Compare the discussion of freemasonry and critique of Halévi in Marcel David, *Fraternité et révolution française* (Paris: Aubier, 1987), 34–37.

43. Ritual in manuscript, B.N. FM Baylot lmpr. 1165; [Par M.D* C***], *Recueil de Discours Moraux* (Geneva, 1782), 67–69, a discourse probably by a woman addressed to the Grande Maitresse, sisters, and brothers.

44. See the eighteenth-century "Statuts des dames" (n. 25 above).

45. *L'Adoption ou la maçonnerie des femmes en trois grades*, 61.

46. Ibid., 54.

47. The *cantique de cloture* can be found in most ritual books, virtually unchanged from one to the next. Other songs varied from lodge to lodge and collection to collection, and often they were written to commemorate one special occasion, but the *cantique de cloture* seems to have become a standard part of the ritual.

48. *L'Adoption ou la maçonnerie des dames. A la Fidelité* (n.p., 1783), B.N. 16 H 618, p. 17.

49. *Esquisse des travaux d'adoption dirigés par les officiers de la loge de la Candeur* (Paris, 1778), 2.

50. "Tableau des frères et soeurs qui suivent l'atelier de la loge de la Sinçerité a l'O . . . de Besançon" (1778), B.N. FM 2 165.

51. Louis Amiable, *Le Franc-Maçonnerie et la magistrature en France à la veille de la Revolution* (Aix, 1894), 21; Régine Robin, "La Loge La Concorde a l'Orient de Dijon" *Annales historiques de la révolution française* 197 (July–September 1969): 433–46.

52. Robin, "La Loge," 434.

53. Suzanne Desan, "Constitutional Amazons: Jacobin Women's Clubs in the French Revolution" in Bryant T. Ragan, Jr., and Elizabeth A. Williams, eds., *Re-Creating Authority in Revolutionary France* (New Brunswick, N.J.: Rutgers University Press, 1992), 11–35.

54. "Tableau des officiers et membres de la R. L. de la Parfaite Amitié a l'O de Toulouse" (1786), reproduced in its entirety in Amiable, *Le Franc-Maçonnerie*, 70–72.

55. On the men, see Lenard R. Berlanstein, *The Barristers of Toulouse in the Eighteenth Century* (Baltimore: Johns Hopkins University Press, 1975), 126–27. In his analysis of the banisters in masonic lodges, Berlanstein concluded that they used the lodges as points of social contact.

56. Robin, "La Loge," 438–39.

57. "Loge de la maçonnerie de femmes; Loge d'adoption," Juigné Collection, vol. 5. 8, pp. 300–359, Archives municipales, Dijon.

58. Guillemain de Saint Victor (n. 26 above), 128–29.

59. Ibid., 129–30.

60. *Esquisse des travaux* (n. 49 above), 18.

61. "Loge de la maçonnerie des femmes."

62. Cissie C. Fairchilds, *Poverty and Charity in Aix-en-Provence, 1640–1789* (Baltimore: Johns Hopkins University Press, 1976), 23.

63. Colin Jones, *Charity and Bienfaisance: The Treatment of the Poor in the Montpellier Region, 1740–1815* (New York: Cambridge University Press, 1982), 76.

64. The figure was defined by the Committee on Mendicity of the constituent assembly and reported in Fairchilds, *Poverty and Charity*, ix. Compare Christine Chapalaine-Nougaret, *Misère et assistance dans le pays de Rennes au xviiie siècle* (Paris: Cid, 1989), 115.

65. G. H. Luquet, *La Franc-Maçonnerie et l'état en France au XVIII siècle* (Paris: Vitiano, 1963), 123–24.

66. M. Thory, *Acta Latomorum* (Paris, 1815), 149.

67. Règlement de la loge de la Concorde, Bibliothèque municipale, Dijon, MS An II, letter of 1781.

68. *Esquisse des travaux*, 41.

69. This statement is from a printed circular done by La Candeur, Paris, and signed by the Duchess de Bourbon (B.N. Baylot FM 2 53, 31 May 1782).

70. The manuscript is signed "Bignon" and dated 1782 from the lodge La Fidelité in Paris (B.N. MS FM 2 76, item no. 38). See chapter appendix under "Paris" for this lodge.

71. [T. C. Frèré de Voltaire], *Esquisse des travaux d'ad option, dirigés par les officiers de la loge de La Candeur* (Leiden, 1778), microfiche, p. 4: "Tout Citoyen s'approche avec confiance du Prince qui l'accueille; l'un oublie son élévation, l'autre n'oublie rien, & tous deux sont égaux par les vertues." Available from IDC.

72. *Manuel des francs-maçons et des franches-maçonnes, nouvelle edition, enrichie des plusieurs cantiques* (Philadelphia, [1791]), 57, 82.

73. *Les francmaçons*, B.N. Y th 30133.

74. *Polichinel, bourgeois de Paris au Grand Orient de France, ou extrait de la planche à tracer du senat maçonnique, 1'an de la lumière veritable 5784, le 3 du neuvième mois* (n.p., 1786), 9.

75. Marcy, *Essai*, 2; 143.

76. M. L'Abbé R-, *Recherches sur les initiations anciennes et modernes* (Amsterdam, 1779), 92, 153–54.

77. *Les Francs-Maçons, plaideurs* (Geneva, 1786), viii

78. Mellor, *Les grandes problèmes*, 115.

79. A similar pattern can be seen in the Netherlands, as revealed in the work of W. W. Mijnhardt. For it and the first women's scientific society in Europe, established in Zeeland in 1785, see Margaret C. Jacob and Dorothée Sturkenboom, "A Women's Scientific Society in the West: The Late Eighteenth-Century Assimilation of Science" *Isis* 94 (June 2003): 217–52.

80. Marcy, *Essai* 2: 115.

81. Ibid.

82. Jean-Claude Madec, "Un siècle de vie maçonnique dans le Barrois, 1767–1856,"*Bulletin Intérieure de la Commission d'Histoire de Grand Orient de France* 2 (November 1971): 7.

83. M. André Rousselle, *La Franc-Maçonnerie à Beauvais* (Beauvais, 1866), 15–16.

84. B.N. FM 2 165, no. 30.

85. For La Française Elue Ecossaise, see Marcy, *Essai*, 2:149; for the Loge L'Amitié, see Thory, *Acta Latomorum*, 121.

86. Charles Bernardin, *Notes pour servir à l'histoire de la Franc-Maçonnerie à Nancy* (Paris: Imprimerie nancéienne, 1910), 176.

87. Marcy, *Essai*, 2: 161.

88. Ibid., 149. See also records dating from 1783 in B.N. FM 2 218; Aulard, "Notes de lecture," 257.

89. On the initial constitutions of the lodges, see Hilaire-Pierre de Loucelles, *Histoire générale de Ia franc-maçonnerie en Normandie 1739–1875* (Dieppe: Emile Delevoye, 1875), 6; Marcy, *Essai*, 2:140. For the 1782 and the 1783 inauguration of the temple; see Loucelles, *Histoire*, 174–75; Marcy, *Essai*, 2: 141, 161. On the Comtesse de Caumont's 1786 discourse, see Marcy, *Essai*, 2: 141, 161. For Saint Louis du Regiment du Roi, see Loucelles, *Histoire*, 6. For the men's lodges, see B.N. FM 2 221.

90. B.N. FM 2 223.

91. Marcy, *Essai*, 2: 161.

92. For the Abbot de Bazinghem's remarks, see Émile LeSueur, *Livres d'Architecture de la Loge La Fidélité a l'O- d'Hesdin* (Paris R. Leroux, 1914), 397. For La Félicité, see Marcy, *Essai*, 2: 141. For La Fidelité, see Jean-André Faucher and Achille Ricker, *Histoire de la franc-Maçonnerie en France* (Paris: Nouvelles Éditions latines, 1967), 156. For the lodge of adoption of Saint-Louis, see Marcy, *Essai*, 2: 142.

93. Jacques Feneant, *Histoire de la Franc-Maçonnerie en Touraine* (Paris: C.L.D.,1981), 88; Doré, "La Maçonnerie des dames," 7.

94. Faucher and Ricker, *Histoire*, 154.

95. For the lodge of adoption founded on the lodge of Saint Louis, see Bemardin, *Notes*; for a reproduction of the tableau, see Faucher and Ricker, *Histoire*, 179. Marcy, *Essai*, 2: 149.

96. Marcy, *Essai*, 2: 149.

97. For the date of La Candeur, see Georg Kloss, *Geschichte der Freimaurerei in Frankreich, 1725–1830* (Darmstadt: J. Jonghaus, 1852), 1: 257. See also *Esquisse des travaux*. The 1778 letter and the 1778–79 correspondence are at B.N. FM 2 S8bis. For the event at Contrat Social, see Loucelles, *Histoire*, 172; for La Fidelité, see Marcy, *Essai*, 2: 153. For the Loge des Neuf-Soeurs, see Loucelles, *Histoire*, 171; Louis Lartigue, "A propos d'un vieux diplôme d'adoption," *Bulletin des Travaux du Suprème Conseil de Belgique* 45 (1901–2): 47; the primary source is signed "Dixmerie, Orateur," and entitled "Mémoire pour la Loge Neuf-Soeurs" (Paris, 1780), B.N. Baylot FM 2 148. For references to Saint-Jean de la Candeur, see *Bulletin du Bibliophile* 4 (April 1847): 308; Marcy, *Essai*, 2: 157–58. For the 1775 list of members of the Loge de Saint-Antoine, see Loucelles, *Histoire*, 171; Kloss, *Geschichte*, 258; for the judgment, see Doré, "La Maçonnerie des dames," 117–18. The Moscow records now at the Grand Orient contain a dossier for Neuf-Soeurs.

98. A. G. Jouast, "La Maçonnerie a Rennes jusqu'en 1789," *Le Monde maçonnique* (December 1859): 475.

99. On the problem, see Marcy, *Essai*, 2: 150; Doré, "La Maçonnerie des dames," 9.

100. For the 1786 tableau, see Faucher and Ricker, *Histoire*, 173; for the 1787 tableau, see Marcy, *Essai*, 152. For the baptism and marriage, see "Registre des deliberations de la loge maçonnique des Coeurs Réunis de Toulouse . . . 1784–1787," 23, Bibliothèque municipale, Toulouse.

101. Feneant, *Histoire*, 86–87.

102. For 1786, see Loucelles, *Histoire*, 6, 176; for 1787, see Marcy, *Essai*, 2: 152.

CONCLUSION

1. Paul Langford, *Englishness Identified: Manners and Character, 1650–1850* (Oxford: Oxford University Press, 2000), 243.

INDEX

ACKNOWLEDGMENTS

Several of the chapters in this book enjoyed earlier lives as essays, now here considerably revised. A version of Chapter 1 appeared in French and Italian and is based on my article, "Freemasonry" in *Le monde des Lumières*, ed. Vincenzo Ferrone et Daniel Roche (Paris: Fayard, 1999). Chapter 2 presents new research, the result of a long-standing interest in the curiously secular quality of masonic almanacs. Chapter 3 appeared in a Dutch publication, *Een Stille leerschool van deugd en goede zeden: vrijmetselarij in Nederland in de 18e en 19e eeuw*, ed. Anton van de Sande en Joost Rosendaal (Hilversum: Verloren, 1995). Chapter 4 began life as "Money, Equality, Fraternity: Freemasonry and the Social Order in Eighteenth-Century Europe," in *The Culture of the Market: Historical Essays*, ed. Thomas L. Haskell and Richard F. Teichgraeber, III (Cambridge: Cambridge University Press, 1993), 102–35. The final chapter, also revised, comes from Janet M. Burke and Margaret C. Jacob, "French Freemasonry, Women, and Feminist Scholarship," *Journal of Modern History* 68, 3 (September 1996): 513–49. I owe Janet M. Burke a big debt of gratitude for her willingness to see it reappear and for the appendix, published in the original and based entirely upon her work.

Always my work is deeply indebted to countless masonic librarians, particularly at the Library of the Grand Lodge in The Hague, who have assisted with great professionalism and alacrity. There Evert Kwaadgras helped graciously and with remarkable efficiency. In Philadelphia the Grand Lodge Librarian, Glenys Waldman, helped unfailingly. The Grand Lodge in London has also become a true friend to scholars. At the Grand Orient in Paris, Pierre Mollier, its librarian, rekindled my interest in freemasonry, as did the new archives returned from Moscow to rue Cadet in December 2000. One small note: in the eighteenth century what we today call Belgium was the Spanish Netherlands, then the Austrian Netherlands, finally French territory after the revolutionaries of the 1790s invaded. In this book it is just always Belgium.

My editor at Penn Press, Jerry Singerman, has proved a diligent and delightful critic.